Unraveling Daniel

John Zavicar III

NEW HARBOR PRESS
RAPID CITY, SD

Zavicar/New Harbor Press
1601 Mt Rushmore Rd, Ste 3288
Rapid City, SD 57701
NewHarborPress.com

Ordering Information:
Quantity sales. Special discounts are available on quantity purchases by corporations, associations, and others. For details, contact the "Special Sales Department" at the address above.

Unraveling Daniel/John Zavicar III. -- 1st ed.
ISBN 978-1-63357-289-8

Contents

Preface

On May 11, 2023 the same night I signed a contract for publishing Unraveling Daniel I was told in a vision that I am to notify all preachers and teachers that they are not to preach or teach another sermon on Daniel or Revelation until they read this book. As I continued to work on the follow-up book, Decoding Revelation, I pondered on how I might be able to accomplish this assigned task that I knew had come from the Holy Spirit. At first, I wondered if the Lord wanted me to send out emails, but this seemed silly because I would not be able to email all preachers and teachers. I knew there would be more direction and guidance to come so I impatiently waited for it.

A little over two weeks later I received my follow-up message. On May 29, I woke up from a deep sleep at 1 am with both my little fingers numb and asleep as I was listening to a worship song with lyrics "singing Hallelujah, Hallelujah." I could possibly explain the pinky finger on one hand being asleep and numb, but I could not at all understand why both were affected. When I woke, I did a scripture search for "fingers" and only one, Daniel 5:5, seemed to provide clues to the meaning of the vision. In that scripture, Daniel documented fingers appearing to write a death sentence for the Babylonian King Belshazzar who had arrogantly rejected and mocked God and Daniel.

I had only heard the song I was hearing in my vision a few times before, so it took a lot of effort and determination to identify it. The song lyrics from "Gratitude" by Brandon Lake were telling me to be bold in my praising of Jesus. In summary, I have a message to deliver about praising Jesus to remove the death sentence of sin; and I am to be bold in presenting and delivering it.

I still wasn't sure what to do, then I was led to consider Matthew 24:14 that quoted Jesus telling his disciples that they were to document the good news of Jesus to spread the message of His gift of salvation throughout the world. It is out of character for me to claim that this book will provide answers to prophecy. However, the fingers writing "You must read, understand, and share this truth" on a wall on the cover of this book, is not only good advice it is in fulfillment of the Holy Spirit's command. I pray that you have a complete understanding of this book.

Understand the message of prophecy and you will see as I have, that God decreed my life, your life, the church, and in summary, all things. God decreed that I would be writing this message to you in this book and all I had to do was accept the challenge and follow. What if I rejected God's decree? I am certain that God had a back-up plan. You also have a choice to either follow the Holy Spirit inside you to accept the gift of salvation or reject Jesus to follow evil to death and destruction. I pray you choose wisely because time is running short, and soon your fate will be sealed for all eternity.

CHAPTER 1

Navigating

I WOKE UP ONE RECENT morning and found myself at the Los Alamos National Laboratory, called LANL for short, where I was hustling and bustling around doing my job. I wasn't completely sure what my job was this day, but I believe I was working in their Security Division because I was dressed in a camouflage outfit and carrying a side firearm. There were people all around me trying to get to their destination at this premier national center for research and development, design, testing, and even production of advanced weapon systems, satellites, and other James Bond-like specialty projects. LANL was always full of people from nations and countries all around the world trying to maneuver through the almost forty square miles of nearly nine-hundred individual facilities with important national security, energy, and other research missions. Dressed in a camouflage uniform and carrying a sidearm weapon meant that I had a job in the portion of the Security Division at LANL with the Protective Force who provided the physical protection of the near 15,000 employees, contractors, and visitors, along with the protection of all facilities, equipment, and associated classified information.

As I stood among this group of mostly visitors at a central gathering area, I was approached by someone I didn't know but who likely recognized my military outfit as someone they could trust to request help from. This unidentified man was

accompanied by another unknown man who obviously was a foreign visitor trying to get to his important meeting at a facility that was several miles away. Getting across the Laboratory was not easy. There were small buses and midsize passenger vans that travelled around the laboratory in response to telephone requests for travel. The most popular location was the Administration Building that had one large conference room that seated over a thousand people, a medium-sized conference room that seated about a hundred attendees, and several smaller group-sized conference rooms. The midsized conference room was where Washington, D.C., politicians and the stakeholders of the many top secret national security projects would typically meet with the scientists and LANL management for updates and project planning.

I hope you don't mind, but prior to completing the details of that gathering center event, I'm going to take you on a sidebar to recall an experience of mine at LANL that you might find interesting. As I wrote this summary, I recalled attending one particularly important national security project meeting at the midsized conference room that left me wanting to quit this rewarding but sometimes frustrating job. Several years before, there had been what was considered by the media and the politicians in Washington, D.C., to be a major security breach at LANL, and I was involved in a project to correct the issue and ensure that top secret national security information was secure. At the start of this morning meeting, Washington, D.C., oversight personnel from a division of government called "Enforcement," walked into the conference room visibly angry, then without saying a word, rudely took their seats as if they had all eaten something bad the evening before that had given them food poisoning. As the Laboratory senior managers politely introduced themselves and briefly touched on the agenda, I observed the visiting oversight personnel appearing even more agitated. I looked around the conference room and recognized the thirty to forty senior level scientists and managers who had been working long hours and weekends for over a year on the project, and they appeared visibly exhausted from their nonstop dedication to the project mission and completion.

Once LANL management completed the meeting formalities, the D.C. oversight manager, an Assistant Secretary of something or another, angrily walked up to the podium and without a welcoming word, started scolding the whole LANL group for not providing them slides twenty-four hours in advance as requested. LANL management politely protested stating that the team had worked well into the night to ensure that project details that were changing every day and sometimes even every hour, were up to the minute. The scolding went on for ten minutes without any consideration of the fact that the tired project workers and managers had spent another entire night addressing the issue. The insensitive and out-of-touch politicians didn't care—they had a paperwork agenda and would stick to it regardless of reasons. The tone of the meeting was set; the tired and overworked LANL scientists were once again the unimportant grunts, and the politicians were the elite, smart, and in charge privileged ones who were once again gracing us with their presence.

What made matters worse is that LANL's so-called "major security issue" paled in comparison to the arrogant misdeeds of a former presidential candidate who was part of the ruling class in Washington, D.C. This well-known politician had for

years intentionally used and maintained an insecure computing system that left the information on it subject to espionage. Knowing the details of LANL's issue and what had been "neglected" by the Washington types for "one of their own," left me somewhat sick to my stomach. But enough of this sidebar; I'll step off my soapbox to get back to the discussion of that visitor I took responsibility for that morning at LANL.

The visitor needed to get to his important meeting, so I looked for a phone to call transportation to arrange a bus to pick him up and take him to his destination. As I surveyed the busy location, I noticed that all the phones were being used by others frantically trying to accomplish the same goal. Apparently, many people were trying to get to their destination that same day and the phone lines that would help make this happen were all tied up and busy. As I scanned the congested area with people scurrying about, I noticed a person completing their call and setting down the phone, so I hurried to that seat and picked up the phone to make the call. The call connected me to a bus driver who I gave instructions to for picking this visitor up and taking him to his destination, then I woke up! Yes, I woke up! Although it seemed real, I was having another vision rather than experiencing this event. I was not back at the Laboratory I had retired from several years before; I was now working for the Lord, and I knew right away that this was another vision to help me complete my current assignment. The Holy Spirit has been providing me "visions" to give me guidance and direction that help me complete Bible investigations.

First, you are probably scratching your head wondering about my "current assignment" and what a *Bible investigation* is, so prior to explaining the meaning of this vision, I will brief you on my current job. For nearly three years I have been getting visions from the Holy Spirit to help me understand Bible scripture that has in the past caused me doubts in the story of Jesus. I professed having faith in Jesus for about thirty years, but deep down I was full of doubt and this doubt kept me from fully committing. Much of my doubt was attributed to the stated authors of the Gospels. The authors of the first four books of the New Testament contained most of what we know about Jesus, but early in church history, some men, referred to as the "early church fathers," claimed these books were written anonymously so they met and debated the origins. Their conclusion that has been accepted by most theologians today as factual, stated that the four anonymous authors were men named Matthew, Mark, Luke, and John. John as the author never gave me heartburn because he was a well-known and a much-written-about disciple of Jesus. However, Matthew, Mark, and Luke as authors were obscure men who seemed very unlikely to be authors, so every time I heard them mentioned, I cringed. Why? Because stories of tradition about these men were created and have since been presented and told as though they are the truth, but there is no evidence to support them. These names for authors never made sense to me as a child, nor have they made sense as I matured into a data-driven scientist and investigator. Although I hear people commonly refer to the "evidence" for their authorship, the words of people that many say prove them as authors, is not evidence, it is considered heresy.

The Holy Spirit had me determine that two of the Gospel authors were not who these "early church fathers" claimed them to be. The result of that first investigation, along with my testimony of coming to faith are presented in my first book

called *Course Corrections to Faith and Identify the Real Gospel Authors.* The Gospel author story accepted by most Christians as the truth was a tale of tradition that crumbled and, based on these results captured in that first book, my doubts in Jesus were eliminated and I became 100% dedicated to Jesus.

Afterward, the Holy Spirit told me I wasn't done by prompting me to take a forensic look at more scripture—the book of Acts. The direction and guidance from the Holy Spirit had me follow-up that first investigation with another that determined that the Gospel of Luke was also misnamed and that meant that three of the four Gospels had been attributed to the wrong people. Having three out of four Gospels misnamed seemed intentional, but I had no proof. As I continued to dig into this mystery, the Lord revealed to me that these three Gospels were intentionally misnamed by false teachers who infiltrated the church, then, as we can verify from history records, ended up calling themselves the "Catholic Church" who forcibly took total control of the church of Jesus Christ. The results of determining who the three Gospel authors were along with the investigation into the fabrication of the story of Matthew, Mark, and Luke now proven to be false, was presented in a follow-up book named *The Early Church Father Catholic Fraud.*

The conclusion of this second investigation provided me answers to most of my questions about the church of Jesus Christ that had bothered me for years. You see, I grew up Catholic and I have several Catholic friends and family members who have, through the years, continually pressured me to commit to joining the Roman Catholic Church (RCC). We proved in that second investigation that the Catholic claim of being the one true church of Jesus Christ is a lie. In addition, we provided evidence that the RCC's claim that anyone rejecting the RCC is condemned to eternal damnation is also a lie. My lingering concern about risking my salvation by pursuing Jesus outside of the RCC was completely resolved. The truth of the RCC's fraud had finally been revealed through evidence in scripture and this set me free from years of bondage to the RCC beliefs.

This is now the third investigation that the Holy Spirit has directed me to undertake. This investigation has been assigned to me to address more questions that exist in the church—those related to prophecy written in the books of Daniel and Revelation. Every time I sat through a sermon addressing the prophecy contained in these two books, the interpretations seemed to hit a raw nerve. Why do theologians claim that the *abomination that causes desolation*—a description of something exceedingly terrible in Daniel 9:24–27—has been fulfilled by a pagan pig roast on the altar in the Jewish temple around 168 BC? This event may have been disgusting but it seems mild compared to past and even current conditions in the church. What makes a pig roast in a temple so horrible that of all the terrible future events God could warn us about, this made the headlines in Daniel's book? What about the numerous churches currently claiming to follow Jesus that accept and even promote the practices of abortion and sexual immorality? These churches must be worse than desecrating an altar in an ancient temple.

Furthermore, countless times I have heard preaching that tells me to keep my eye out for and that I should wait for a future rapture, tribulation, and an appearance by a great antichrist—but according to scripture this makes no sense. John, the disciple of Jesus and author of the fourth Gospel, who also wrote some letters, told us during the start of the church that

it was full of antichrists, and they were destroying the church (1 John 2:18–19, 4:3; 2 John 1:7). It certainly doesn't sound like a future big deal when the problem was widespread at the beginning of the church, so why then are Christians looking up and out for an antichrist? Current interpretations don't seem to make sense, and this causes more doubts in the story of Jesus. I'll get a little more into this when we deep dive into the book of Daniel.

With this background, I can now explain the meaning of the vision. Not all the visions I receive are easily understood, but this one was because it was provided by God as an answer to a prayer that I made the night before. I had a dilemma to deal with as I started to assemble the message of this third book—How do I, a data-driven engineer and investigator, write an interesting book rather than a dry and stale report that captures the results of another investigation? A pastor friend of mine, who by the way is also a brilliant chemist professor, read my first book and his evaluation stated, "I could tell it is written by an engineer." Does this sound like a complement to you? You are probably laughing because you know some engineers. I fit the mold of a typical engineer with a brain for math, but I am a person with limited creativity. Give me a scientific or math problem and I'm very comfortable but ask me to draw something or create an interesting story and you'll laugh at my ineptitude and frustration. My pastor friend followed up the "engineer" comment by telling me "I'm using some of the material from your book in my Sunday sermons," so I immediately recognized that he was trying to soften the hit I took for being an engineer. God provided me puzzle-solving abilities but very little creativity skills and this was apparent in my first book.

Based on my recognition of my creativity limitations, I prayed for help as I assembled the second book, and I received it. How do I know? Two very important artistically gifted people in my life—my wife, Karen, and daughter, Courtney, read the second book and congratulated me for writing an introduction that caught their attention to motivate them to continue reading. They went on to explain, "If a book doesn't capture my attention in the first few pages, I put it down, and I wanted to continue reading your second book." That put pressure on me to write an introduction for this third book that would get your attention and encourage you to continue reading it. I struggled, then turned to prayer. As always, my prayer was answered when the next day I woke up with the vision of LANL that I opened this first chapter with.

I immediately knew that this vision was intended to be an interesting story for readers to help encourage them to continue reading; but, if my prayer was to be fully answered, it also had to have a key message embedded in it that the Holy Spirit wanted me to present—the reason for this book. I didn't have to ponder this vision much because the message was very clear from the start. First, the job I was tasked with in that vision was to assist a person who was clearly a "foreigner." Why a foreigner? Because a foreigner would not be familiar with LANL—he did not know his way around. Hmm . . . my books are about learning the truth about Jesus to help nonbelievers find and follow Jesus—they are visiting their faith and having doubts, so they need help—they are foreigners to Jesus.

The assembling area where I picked that foreigner up is like the church—it's a very confusing place with people scurrying around. Is the church really a confusing place? Look at the

church from the outside as a foreigner searching for Jesus and what do you see? A crazy and confused bunch of people who call themselves "Christians" all scurrying around to various denominations of churches that seem to have different messages about Jesus. Scripture has been sprinkled with tradition and various wild and untrue interpretations, making it confusing; and there are multiple factions and denominations of churches. To an outsider, these nutty Christians have a range of beliefs like walking into an ice cream store and choosing your flavor. If you want sexual immorality and abortion approval you can find it in the church. If you want a Jesus who provides you a bunch of rules, regulation, and formality to follow to get to heaven, you can find that too. Choose your Jesus, then find a church that will best suit you. Move to a new location and try to find a church that sticks only to the words of Jesus rather than a long list of rules and beliefs provided by an affiliated oversight organization—and it's a very difficult endeavor.

What is the help being provided to this foreigner—the bus ride. The transportation to the meeting with Jesus is considered the path you will take to get to Jesus. You might never find the bus, or you might get on the wrong bus. You might get on the bus and get off to lose your way. My job was to get this foreigner on the right bus that would take him to Jesus. My books are helping to resolve the confusing mess of the church; I have been asked to find the truth in various portions of scripture and present it. My investigation results are eliminating the tradition that permeated through scripture and the church so that the truth about Jesus and his church are revealed, and this will help people find the true Jesus.

There are many buses that can take people for a ride at LANL, but only the *right bus* will get this foreigner to his destination. I hope you noticed that I never saw that foreigner get on the bus. This too has a meaning I need to explain. I connected someone to the right bus and the bus was on the way to pick him up, so my work had ended but what happened next? I don't know because I didn't see what that foreigner did next. Did he get on the right bus? Did he take the wrong bus or get off at the wrong location? Like I have written, there are many churches, and that foreigner could have been sidetracked to end up at one of the churches participating in pagan worship or allowing sexual immorality and sin. Yes, I arranged the bus to help this person find the truth in Jesus, but that didn't mean that he accepted the ride. Like that foreigner who had a choice, those reading my investigation reports also have a choice.

I can present the data, but I can't force anyone to read or accept it; that decision is up to you. What you do with the messages I write to try to clean up the mess of the story of Jesus and the church is up to those who read it. Many will remain in the confused area and will not make their connection to Jesus and then one day they will die, and it will be too late. Others will look for a church that provides a message that allows them to continue in sin and they will go for a ride on the wrong bus that will never get them to Jesus. Still others may get on the bus and be on their way to meet Jesus, then decide to get off the bus at the wrong stop, thereby never getting to know him.

In summary, the Holy Spirit has given me a job to help you find Jesus and the results of this investigation are the ways the Lord has me reaching out to you. The Gospel author investigation exposed the story of tradition that replaced the names

of the eyewitnesses who documented the life and mission of Jesus. When tradition is stripped away, the real author story pointed straight to Jesus and a lot of the confusion in the Gospels was cleared up. The identification and exposing of the fraud committed by the founders of the RCC revealed how the false teachers that Jesus and the disciples warned us all about, grew into an evil entity that took over the church. Our results pointed you away from false teachers and corrupt churches and provided the right bus to the true Jesus. The summary you will read in this book about the prophecy in Daniel will highlight how God accurately predicted the arrival of his Son and the entire future of the church. Through prophecy, you will see the accurate fulfillment of prophecy that told us the time of Jesus would not be a time of peace. In addition, the confusing mess that theologians have told you is the meaning of Daniel will be proven to be more false stories of tradition. You will find the message of prophecy written in Daniel to be very clear and focusing 100% on Jesus.

CHAPTER 2

More Messy Church Details

*T*HE FIRST CHAPTER DESCRIBED the winding, treacherous, and confusing path people searching for faith in God must travel to find the truth in Jesus. For the last three years my mission has been to sort through scripture and analyze the details to help unravel the truth and separate it from the tradition that has liberally been injected into the church. This chapter is about that tradition that has spread throughout the church and has been normalized as generally accepted theology. There are two terms I need to define in that previous sentence prior to moving on, *the church* and *generally accepted theology. The church* is not a building—it is the preachers, teachers, and those sitting in the audience who listen to scripture —the Word of God. *The church* is the entity that God gave his people as the bridge to find, be with, and grow in Jesus. *Generally accepted theology* is anything outside of scripture that is taught as though it is the Word of God. We discussed two prime examples of generally accepted theology in the last chapter—the renamed Gospel authors Matthew, Mark, and Luke, and the seven-year period of the antichrist, tribulation, and rapture. Both these beliefs are *not scriptural*—they were not eyewitness testimony written by the apostles; these are stories of tradition created by men.

Most Christians with rock-solid beliefs hold on tight to these unproven stories of tradition and don't like it when someone

claims them as far-fetched tales. Since the Holy Spirit has been leading me to the evidence in scripture that proves some generally accepted theology to be from false teachers, you probably have a pretty good idea of where I'm leading you. I want to welcome you to my world of proving the truth in scripture that has resulted in me being rejected by the church. This rejection has caused consistent turmoil in my life starting approximately two years ago when I concluded that the Gospels had been misnamed. The rejection of me and my conclusions kicked up a notch when we proved the RCC founders committed church fraud. Most recently, determining the truth about Daniel's prophecy has the church in a wild tizzy and on the attack. When we started proving and claiming that prophecy was not validating the theory of the seven-year antichrist, tribulation, and rapture, you would have thought I declared Jesus to be dead.

I continually analyzed my dilemma of providing results that proved Jesus as the truth, but with a rejected and ridiculed message. Whenever I tried to share the good news that the truth of Jesus was being revealed to me through scripture, I found that the church did not want to hear about it. I continually prayed for the Lord to help me with the friction between me and the church and, in response, I received help from the Holy Spirit in the form of visions and answers to prayer. However, I had trouble understanding the guidance and direction the Holy Spirit was trying to give me. Over the last three years, I've had numerous visions and some I immediately understood, but others—including the ones related to church rejection—took a fair amount of time and effort to unravel. The visions related to understanding and addressing the rejection from the church I was facing was one of those messages that I didn't immediately grasp. It turns out that this was intentional—God had a message for me.

The Lord took me on this painful journey of rejection to make an important point. As I was trying to deal with church rejection, I was having trouble understanding some aspects of Daniel. Specifically, the events and visions of Daniel did not seem to be presented chronologically yet they seemed to be documented in a haphazard manner. In addition, there were passages in Daniel that seemed to indicate that Daniel served under a king named Darius that nobody has been able to find historical records for. Theologians have generated various theories to address this discrepancy but there is no proof or evidence to support any of them. In summary, I was struggling with my issue of visions and rejections while I was trying to understand Daniel's visions and some confusing passages he wrote.

In the end, the Holy Spirit revealed to me that my process of trying to understand my visions to resolve my issue of rejection by the church was the key to understanding these confusing aspects of the book of Daniel I was having trouble unraveling. The rest of this chapter will help you understand the turmoil caused by my rejection and the process I went through to resolve it. That will set the stage for the next chapter that will present how, through this journey, the Holy Spirit helped me resolve my grief and dilemma then apply my experience to Daniel's life and book. The Holy Spirit had a very important message for me to learn and this message unraveled hidden aspects of the book of Daniel that had me resolve the order of Daniel's book and the mystery of King Darius.

The rest of this chapter will walk you through my turmoil that started with the Gospel author naming. Finding the names of the Gospel authors through scripture analysis was no small feat and the results excited me. As expected, when I talked about Jesus and my results—which was constantly—my nonbeliever friends started to avoid me. Unexpectedly, my Christian family members and friends had the same reaction, but their rejection came with some of the following comments:

- "Who are you to believe that the Gospel authors aren't who everybody else over 2,000 years says they are?"
- "Do you think you're smarter than everyone else who has looked at the history and evidence to determine that Matthew, Mark, and Luke are the authors?"
- "What makes you so special that God chose you to reveal this?"

I continually prayed for help to deal with this rejection and asked God for guidance on what I should do. Should I quit talking about it? Should I use another tactic? I was confused and lost. I had 100% confidence in our results, but the church had 0% confidence in them.

Then, as the first book was with the publisher being edited, I received the following vision:

> June 2021—I was hiking in the woods I crossed paths with Pastor Skip. I wanted to talk to him for guidance on the book, but I tried and wasn't permitted. As we passed each other by I said hi and wanted to continue talking to him, but because he was with his family and I didn't think

he had much time with his family, I didn't say anything. I walked a bit farther then realized I should have said something, so I turned around and went back to find him, but he had already gone down the path. I was not going to have an opportunity to bring up the book message to him.

I needed someone to have a theological discussion with me and I felt as though the Lord was telling me I needed to reach out to Pastor Skip. We had moved and were now living approximately 1,600 miles away from our church, therefore, I tried to contact Pastor Skip through a few phone calls. This proved unsuccessful, so when I couldn't get past the firewall of this very large church, I sent Skip an email. In response to my email, as expected, I received a welcoming email from an associate pastor named Isaac.

Isaac was very pleasant in his introduction email, but after I emailed him back describing the work I was doing and my conclusions about the Gospel authors, Isaac didn't respond. After a few more attempts to explain my investigations and results to Isaac through additional emails without getting a response, I concluded that Isaac was working for that church, but he was not working for the Lord, so I stopped trying. I couldn't help but wonder about Isaac's impact on others—How many other people had tried to connect to Jesus through that church and been routed to Isaac only to be ignored? This thought pained me, and I wondered how frequently this happened in large churches who had effective pastors bringing people to faith in Jesus but had underlings working for them who were destroying their

work as they walked behind them. A large church is wonderful, but without proper management and oversight, those hired to help the large church could be doing more harm than good.

Afterward, the rejection of Christian friends and family picked up in intensity; then, a few months later, I received the following vision:

> Oct 16, 2021—Woke up from a nap knowing we had to physically go to church so that we can grow in the Holy Spirit.

There is no confusion about this message, we had finally settled down and had no plans on leaving the area, so it was time for me and Karen to find and physically attend a local church rather than try to stay connected to the church many miles away. I searched online and found a church about twenty-five miles away and then we immediately started physically attending services every week.

I felt welcome at our new church and although I missed Skip's sermons, we started calling this church home. The first book was with the publisher, and I was now deep into the study for the second book's results. My welcome at this new church seemed to wear off quickly after I began discussing the investigations and results; I began getting the cold shoulder from those in the church. I still couldn't understand why results that proved the story of Jesus to be true were causing such heartburn in Christians. I knew my results verified Jesus as the Son of God so I thought that *all* Christians would be excited about these results—but they weren't. Now I was experiencing rejection from Christians in my personal life *and* those in our new church. All

I wanted was a Jesus follower who was excited to go over the details of my work and this did not at all seem unreasonable. Throughout my career, I documented reports that contained investigation conclusions and others eagerly reviewed results and provided feedback. "What is so different with Christians?" I wondered.

I was so frustrated and disgusted with the rejection of fellow Christians at our new church that I even considered finding a different one or returning to online feeding of the soul with our previous church, but then I received the following vision:

> March 15, 2022—Skip is at our place and he is sitting on the bed talking to me and Karen. We have church on the TV and I'm trying to sing the worship songs, but he's sitting in the way so I can't see the words. I'm frustrated about it and trying to look around him but I can't seem to see the words. He mentions that he's going to Ghana on a missionary trip.

I summarized from this vision that I was blocked from reaching Skip and it is his fault because he had put into place the bureaucracy that rejected me, but I was not to hold this against him because he was furthering the Word and spreading the gospel. Also in the vision, I was watching the service on TV, but the worship words were being hidden from me. This aspect of the vision reinforced to me that watching the service from home was not the answer and leaving this church was not what God wanted.

Consider that when I was a Christian full of doubts, I never had any issues with Christians or the church, but now that I'm working for the Lord, I'm faced with continual rejection from all sides. I continued to feel more isolated and had nobody to share my joy of investigation results and the newfound confidence in the story of Jesus that the results brought me. Then, the Holy Spirit helped Karen to see that my visions were coming from God when I had a vision to sell our house; we followed it, and purchased a residence nearby that we are both happy and content with. I capture the complete details of this vision in the next book about Revelation prophecy, but in summary, all our prayers were answered as we followed the Lord's directions and guidance. With Karen on board, I felt a bit of relief but the rejection from others was still on my mind 24/7. Then, I received the following vision that shook me up, and, in a way, made me laugh:

> May 17, 2022—I didn't think it was possible and I'm not sure why, but this morning the message was "bite your tongue." I bit my WHOLE tongue. I kept hearing the verses from church song, ". . . and I stand with my hands lifted high, oh God, the battle belongs to you."

This was not a small bite of my tongue—it was as though the Holy Spirit pulled my tongue out of my mouth as far as it could go then had me intentionally bite it. I didn't realize a tongue could go out of a mouth that far and it shocked me! At first, I thought the meaning of this vision was obvious—the Holy Spirit was telling me, "Shut up, John; and quit talking to people because you're getting them mad and it's starting to get to you." I tried being silent for about a month and it was difficult. Then, the first book was issued, and the results of the second book were about ready to go to a publisher. I wanted to share the messages, so I started reevaluating my interpretation of this series of visions that had not had any positive results yet.

Upon reflection of my experiences and visions, I realized that the Lord had me investigate the sources of my doubts, resolve them, and write books to provide the messages. I asked myself, "When have you ever read in scripture that Jesus told his followers to be silent?" I think you know the answer to that—never! Not once could I recall a preacher ever telling people to be silent about faith in Jesus —we are not supposed to be silent, we are supposed to share the Word. I reconsidered the trail of visions including biting my tongue and thought that maybe the Lord was just telling me that I was going to experience pain every time I spoke about the results.

After the first book came out in June 2022, I talked to an associate pastor at our church about the results and when I did, he seemed interested, so I agreed to bring him a copy to read. I brought the associate pastor a copy of the first book the following week and he happened to be on vacation, so I gave it to the lead pastor who showed no interest in it but agreed to give it to the associate pastor. About three months later, I checked in with the associate pastor who stated he hadn't yet had a chance to look at it. At the same time, the results of the second book were causing issues between me and the Catholics in my life. In addition, with the second book at the publisher, I was deep into the third investigation looking at prophecy. This was the last straw for many in the church.

First, I attacked the Gospel authors; then, I attacked the Catholics; and, now, I'm presenting the story of the future end times seven-year period of the antichrist, tribulation, and rapture as a fable. This apparently appeared as though I was again attacking the faith of many Christians. The ridicule and rejection I experienced were so profound that one day near the bottom of my despair, I suggested to my family that maybe I should isolate myself and get an apartment to allow me to investigate and write in peace—I was serious. Then, as I dug deeper into Daniel, I came across a passage that provided me some peace:

> In the first year of Belshazzar king of Babylon,
> Daniel had a dream, and visions passed through
> his mind as he was lying in bed. He wrote down
> the substance of his dream. (Daniel 7:1)

This simple verse of scripture gave me comfort to know that I wasn't crazy. Just like Daniel described, I wake up with a dream, vision, or words in my head, then, because it is early in the morning, I lie in bed receiving follow-up visions and ponder what I have been told to try to understand the meaning. After a short while of pondering the message, I get up to pray and glorify God while asking the Holy Spirit for guidance and direction—then the words flow into my head, and I write. When I read Daniel's accounting of his vision, I thanked the Lord for the insight! Just for the few of you who might read arrogance into this last summary, I didn't compare myself to Daniel, I simply claimed that his description of his visions helped me understand mine.

My peace was short-lived as I was again confronted by Christians who asked me, "So you really think that of all the brilliant minds that have studied prophecy, God is revealing this information to you?" I prayed every day, but it didn't seem like I was getting an answer; then, I received the following vision:

> October 12, 2022—I was starting a new job at some place. I was in early and hanging out in an office talking to some girl who I was getting along with, and she was making me feel comfortable. She was kind of quirky but cute and personable. It was as though I was starting a new career and I was waiting to go into the manufacturing facility. We were in another girl's office and I didn't know it. The girl arrived and stood next to me hinting that I was in her seat at her desk. I asked her if I was in her office and she said "Yes," so after a few moments I got up and figured it was time to go to work. As I was leaving, I turned back around and said to the quirky girl, "By the way, what's your name?" She smiled and said, "August." I smiled back and said, "That's my birthday," and left.

I immediately thought that through this vision, the Lord was telling me that I was going to change jobs in a while, and this excited me. I couldn't wait for the prospect of leaving my investigations and authorship of books behind. A remote thought of mine was that I might even be called back home to heaven in

August 2023, and if this was the Lord's plan, I welcomed this outcome too.

A new job meant no more results and rejection, but I had to accept the fact that my interpretation of this vision could be wrong—I wasn't certain about this interpretation, so I wrote it down to revisit later. Then, a few months later, I received a series of flash visions:

> January 10, 2023—I am getting my guns ready. In my vision, I am loading clips into my weapons.

> January 12, 2023—I am looking at the battery gauge on our golf cart and it blips then goes dead—the power goes out.

> January 13, 2023—There is an ongoing battle. Soldiers, who I believe are on the opposing side, but I can't tell, pass me by on a small barge and tell me that I should go to the lodge or center where troops are being gathered and deployed. They didn't seem to know what side I was on.

It seemed obvious to me that a battle was coming, or that I was already in a battle. I certainly felt that I was in a battle, but I couldn't help but wonder what the Lord was trying to tell me—I wasn't quite sure. Was there going to be a struggle in the world I needed to prepare for or was the Lord giving me more advice about the battles I was facing in the church? Soldiers wanted me fighting, but they weren't quite sure whose side I was on. Hmm . . . I couldn't figure it out, so I wrote these visions down and continued investigating scripture while waiting for more clues.

About three or four weeks after this series of visions in January 2023, Karen's mother who is also a devout Christian, came for a visit and we started talking about visions and their meaning. Karen's mom revealed that, a while ago, she had received a vision of an invading army battling people in Detroit. Karen added that, in the past, she too had the same vision of an invading military force, but it wasn't in Detroit, it was in New York City. Their visions caused me to recapture the ones that seemed to tell me I was in a battle or the battle was coming. We couldn't determine the meaning of it all, so I went on to reference the job vision as an example of another one I couldn't understand the meaning of. As I retold that vision, I stated the words *August* and *my birthday* and realized that this was not my birthday because there was no date given, so it must be a clue to solving it.

I immediately recalled the following earlier vision I had received several months before:

> July 1, 2022—I was told in a vision to not skip
> any verses and read each word carefully.

I realized I was not paying attention to the details of that vision, so I considered that this vision may apply to my current work on Daniel. I walked to my desk and went straight to the book of Daniel, and I turned to chapter eight. There I saw that there were "27" verses in chapter eight and I said, "Hmm, that's really interesting because my birthday is on the 27th." This verse read:

> I, Daniel, was worn out. I lay exhausted for several days. Then I got up and went about the king's business. I was appalled by the vision; it was beyond understanding. (Daniel 8:27)

I knew right away that the Lord had taken me on a journey to discuss these visions of war with Karen and her mom to get me back to that vision to help me understand it.

I wasn't getting a new job—I was being told to continue what I was already doing—"the king's business." I needed to quit whining about the job I had even though, like Daniel, I was worn out and exhausted from investigating and, many times, I have found the meanings of my visions to be beyond comprehension—I couldn't understand them. My job is to go about doing the king's business and let the king worry about the details. As a side note, file this verse in your memory because it will apply to clearing up our understanding of Daniel. Daniel certainly had trouble understanding the meaning of his visions—he admitted this fact in verse 8:27.

I have been assigned a job to do, so I should quit worrying about the battles that I have been fighting. Do my job and leave the rest up to the Lord! Returning to my experience of biting my tongue with the vision having me sing the words *"oh God, the battle belongs to you"* suddenly meant something that was very valuable. The battle was not mine although I was trying to make it mine! Now, I understood that the battle belonged to the Lord, and I was to continue to investigate and report.

I never did hear back from the associate pastor who had agreed to read the first book and now the second book was getting issued. I'm trained to read body language and I started noticing that I was being avoided in church. The church changed practices to pray for half an hour at the end of each service for the Holy Spirit to speak to those in the congregation, but I didn't need this half hour because the Holy Spirit was speaking to me every day. I had tried to communicate to this church what I was hearing, but nobody would listen. I guess they were interested in the Holy Spirit but didn't want to hear about the Holy Spirit in me! I sent several pastors emails and left phone messages, but all my attempts to connect to the church staff fell on deaf ears. In February 2023, I asked the associate pastor if he had read my book and he told me it was sitting unopened on his desk, but he hoped to get to it soon. Frustrated, I walked away as I asked him to give it to somebody in the church who might care to read it. A few weeks later, at a Saturday evening service, the lead pastor made an obvious lame attempt to avoid me, and I wondered if it was time to find a new church.

I received my answer a few days later through the following vision:

> February 28, 2023—The pastor was standing by me, and I tried to get his attention by tapping on his shoulder and tugging on his hand. In response, he took a swing at me and missed, so I said, "You're lucky you missed," and walked away.

This isn't a confusing message—I was considered a nuisance at this church and the Lord was telling me it was time to shake the dust off my feet and move on. Consider what has happened now at two very well-attended churches being taught

by Jesus-loving pastors—I have been rejected—for proving the story of Jesus to be true! In summary, the Holy Spirit is working with me to deliver messages that point to Jesus but, at the same time, the messages are separating me from Christians and the church.

I felt alone and prayed for more direction. I prayed to the Lord that if my books helped one person find Jesus, then all the struggles and hard work was worth it. About this time, I saw the first evidence of this success and I was greatly encouraged. In addition, Karen was realizing my struggles and started to thoroughly research what I was reporting. She bought a different study Bible and started rereading my first and second books. Then, as I was trying to resolve that issue of Daniel I was contending with, I received the answer to my rejection—and this pointed me directly to the resolution of my Daniel questions—the reason for me providing this long journey.

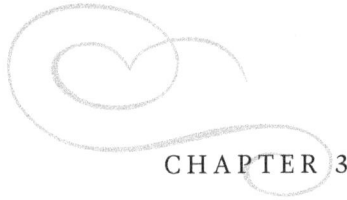

CHAPTER 3

Weeds, Trees, and Understanding

THE LAST CHAPTER SUMMARIZED the reaction of others to the directions and guidance I received from the Holy Spirit. In summary, I have been claiming investigation results that eliminated my long-standing doubts by *proving* the story of Jesus to be true, but Christians and the church were treating me as though I had claimed the story of Jesus was a fabrication. I predicted that my nonbelieving friends would start to distance themselves from me, but the reactions of my Christian friends, family, and those in the church, took me by surprise. I had expected that those following Jesus would welcome my results, be excited to hear about them, and want to go over the data to evaluate the findings. But this is not what happened; the response to my books was opposite of my expectation. There was no joy to be found in my results; there was only the rejection I presented in the last chapter.

The vision of the pastor taking a swing at me had me looking for another church and, in answer to my prayer, I found a church within twenty-five miles of us in the opposite direction. Being a bit gun-shy from the reactions of those in the church thus far, I wrote the pastor of that large church informing him of the messages I was being asked by the Holy Spirit to deliver

to see whether I would get a response or again be ignored. I almost started this next sentence starting with the word *surprisingly,* but when considering answers to prayers and visions from the Holy Spirit, the results should not surprise anyone. Unlike my previous experiences, Pastor Dave of Calvary Chapel Melbourne personally took the time to respond to my email with an invite to the next service that would address a subject called "apologetics." I hadn't heard of the subject of apologetics, so I researched and found it to be the theological branch of Christianity that defends and proves the truth of Christian doctrine. Pastor Dave's email response stated that this service should be of interest to me, so he had obviously carefully considered my email and thoughtfully responded. I wasn't familiar with the theological field of apologetics, but this pastor recognized the connection between my work and this branch of Christian study.

I couldn't wait for the service because the more I looked at apologetics, the more I felt that my results fit into this study branch of theology. Like others in the field of apologetics, the Holy Spirit was working with me to find the truth of scripture. I thought, "Wow, did the Lord take me on a path here or what?" Soon after attending the sermon on apologetics, I was led by the Holy Spirit to an old saying, "Can't see the forest for the trees." This common statement is best explained by a summary presented at https://grammarbrain.com/cant-see-the-forest-for-the-trees/:

> The idiom *can't see the forest for the trees* means that the parts are distracting you from comprehending the whole. You can't see the

entirety as you are preoccupied with the details and overlook the bigger picture or the end goal. In this context, it signifies the trees are obscuring the fact that they collectively form a forest. Figuratively, it means you are lost in the maze of details and cannot discern that there is something larger behind what's apparent.

I knew right away that the Holy Spirit was telling me that the forest was the big picture, and the forest I was dealing with was Jesus. With Jesus as the forest, the trees become scripture, preachers, and teachers of the Word—all comprising the church; I previously had trouble finding Jesus because I was lost in the trees. I considered that the Holy Spirit might be telling me that my work will help those who were like me and had a problem finding Jesus through the confusion of the church. Until my investigation results solidified my faith in Jesus, I was unable to "find the forest for the trees" and I was to share my experience with others. This made sense, but it still didn't explain to me the rejection I was experiencing from the church.

Then, during early March 2023, I turned to prayer with a walk on the beach to admire God's creation and seek an answer. As I walked, in a flash the Lord pointed me to the parable of the weeds, so I started to consider this. I knew this parable by heart; and I remembered that Jesus had stated that evil people would plant weeds among the good plants, but the weeds were to be left alone until harvesttime because removing them might destroy the good crop among the weeds. From the New King James Version of the Bible, we have the following:

Another parable He put forth to them, say-ing: "The kingdom of heaven is like a man who sowed good seed in his field; but while men slept, his enemy came and sowed tares among the wheat and went his way. But when the grain had sprouted and produced a crop, then the tares also appeared. So the servants of the owner came and said to him, 'Sir, did you not sow good seed in your field? How then does it have tares?' He said to them, 'An enemy has done this.' The servants said to him, 'Do you want us then to go and gather them up?' But he said, 'No, lest while you gather up the tares you also uproot the wheat with them. Let both grow together until the harvest, and at the time of harvest I will say to the reapers, "First gather together the tares and bind them in bundles to burn them, but gather the wheat into my barn."' (Matthew 13:24–30)

The light bulb went on—I was dealing with evil forces who had corrupted scripture and/or its interpretation and they had planted weeds in the Word of God. My job, per the directions and guidance I was receiving from the Holy Spirit through my visions and in answer to prayer, was to remove the weeds. However, through this parable, the Lord was telling me to leave the weeds alone, so I had a conflict.

At the time I was reviewing the parable of the weeds, as I mentioned, I had received some positive feedback from the first book—it was helping a few lost souls to find Jesus and put their faith in him. The light bulb suddenly went on. The parable of the weeds *applied* to the church and my fellow Christians who didn't see the weeds, and *not* to those who already have strong faith in Jesus. Pointing out the weeds in scripture to people who didn't see the weeds, and really didn't want to see them, was simply confusing them. They were the soldiers on that barge who couldn't determine whose side of the battle of faith I was on. By me pointing out the weeds, they wondered if I was working for Jesus or working for the devil. Like I said, they couldn't see the weeds and didn't want to see them so, when I pointed the weeds out to these Christians, it was messing with their faith. I was doing more harm to them than good. Approaching them with my message was just frustrating and confusing them because they didn't need help finding Jesus— they had already found Jesus and they were on the right bus— hence their rejection. However, on the flip side, the positive feedback from those who were like I previously was with my doubts were benefitting from the removal of the weeds. When they tried to believe in Jesus, like me, all they saw were the weeds, so it helps them to have me pull them out so that they could see the good crop, the living water, and fruit from the vine—the truth of Jesus. These people needed help to get the right bus to take them to Jesus and me removing the weeds was helping them.

The biting of my tongue became clear because I now knew that the Lord was telling me I would experience pain when I spoke until I figured out *who* I was supposed to be speaking to. The lyrics of the song telling me that it was the Lord's battle now made sense. The Lord was telling me, "I got this—so leave me to handle it." The vision in January 2023 that had me

putting clips in my gun was letting me know I was in a spiritual war that was going to get heated and intense. The battery on my golf cart went dead because there were times when this ongoing war would drain all my energy. It turns out that this already happens frequently!

To close out this section explaining how I had finally resolved the issue of my rejection, the Lord told me this morning that I had made the connection and congratulated me for finally figuring it out. Last night when I went to bed, I knew that this morning I would be making the final changes to the message of visions and rejection written about in these introductory chapters to this book. At 1:07 a.m., I woke up biting my tongue for the second time, however, this experience was different from the first violent bite. This bite hurt a bit, but it wasn't nearly as dramatic and profound as the last bite that frightened me nearly a year ago. Upon reflection, the meaning of this is very clear. Last year, the pain was undiagnosed, and it was brutal. As of now, the help I received from the Holy Spirit through visions and prayer has greatly reduced the pain. As I continue "doing the king's business," I will still experience pain, but the pain from rejection is now gone.

Everything quickly made sense, but we're not through yet—remember, I said there was a message in this process of addressing my rejection that provided me a key to unravel the book of Daniel? The title of this chapter has three portions; we addressed *the trees* and *the weeds,* but we still haven't addressed *understanding.* Understanding turns out to be the key that opens the door to Daniel. Let me first provide a foundation for "understanding." As I stated, many of my visions are quickly understood and I address them immediately—like the biting of my tongue last night. However, like those other visions I described throughout my process of trying to figure out why the rejection was directed at me, some visions require a lot of pondering, praying, and continuous reevaluation to help me to understand what I am to learn.

Daniel emphasized understanding in his book. We've already mentioned the word *understand* numerous times in the previous chapters of this book, but let me emphasize the importance of that word. I searched for the word *understand* in scripture using www.biblegateway.com and found 278 references to it throughout the Bible's sixty-six books. The very short book of Daniel with only twelve chapters in it, referenced *understanding* twenty-three times and that put it in fifth place for the total mentions of it. Do you think God wanted Daniel to carefully ponder and understand the message he was providing him? I hope you answered yes!

Understanding the Holy Spirit and his visions was important to Daniel, and he emphasized it repeatedly. Also, and most important, you must understand that "understanding visions" might take some time and effort because this understanding is not always intuitive. It took me a long time to understand my visions, therefore, you can only imagine how difficult it was for Daniel to understand his visions that provided a very complex message. I was dealing with rejection; Daniel was dealing with the entire future of the church and the coming of the Messiah. You get the picture? If it took me a year and several visions to understand a simple message; Daniel needed much more time and effort to understand his complex message. The Lord knew this and even told him this in one of his visions (Daniel 12:9).

Let me emphasize the importance of understanding this concept of understanding visions by recapping a discussion I had with a nonbelieving friend. We recently had visiting friends tag along with us to our church's Saturday evening service. After the service, we stopped at a local diner and started up a conversation about the service and sermon and, somehow, the subject of visions came up. I captured my recent experiences and emphasized the difficulty I sometimes had interpreting visions, but then emphasized that, over time, I figured out the message. I compared this to my review of Daniel that indicated it took a lifetime for Daniel to understand his much more complex visions.

My friend listened patiently to my summary, then at the end stated:

> "What you are telling me proves that God does
> not exist. If God were giving you visions, you
> would understand them immediately; therefore,
> you are having dreams and not visions from God
> . . . I don't believe that there is a God."

I was a bit shocked but, after considering what he said, the light bulb turned on in my head. Unless someone has had to interpret dreams and visions from the Holy Spirit, they would not understand how difficult the process is. The Lord wanted me to go through my long-drawn-out process of determining my visions so that I could apply it to the book of Daniel to help me figure out confusing aspects of Daniel's book, while at the same time providing you proof of the power of the Holy Spirit to work in all of us through visions. I understood how my friend could conclude that if God exists and is all-powerful, he would, by nature of his deity, make his messages clear from the start. However, the error in that conclusion is that God is dealing with the human minds of his creation and our simple brains need time and continual prompting to learn. As humans with free will, we keep doing the same stupid things over and over again while expecting different results. Could I have, or even should I have, understood the message of my visions earlier? Of course, the answer is yes, but I didn't—it took time. It made sense that my unbelieving friend thought visions from the Lord should be self-explanatory, but my experiences had helped me understand that in reality it's a very different and difficult process.

I compared my visions to Daniel's visions and considered how complex his were as compared to mine. The Holy Spirit provided Daniel visions that captured the *entire future* of the church—including the arrival of the Messiah and the details of his mission. Imagine, having visions and trying to understand a message of the entire future of the church together with the story of Jesus—I can't conceive of a more complex sequence of visions. Knowing this, do you think Daniel immediately understood his visions or do you think it took a long time for Daniel to put it all together? It turns out that we don't have to guess the answer to these questions because Daniel told us in his book.

Daniel's book is not at all presented chronologically—this is obvious. But, knowing this presents the million-dollar question—if it isn't chronological, how did Daniel present his life story? At this time, we will walk you through Daniel's book chapter by chapter to let you see how Daniel finally understood the pieces of the spiritual future puzzle near the end of his life.

Then and only then was Daniel able to assemble his visions in a coherent presentation. We unlock the keys to Daniel by considering his understanding of his visions presented in the following high-level summary:

1. Chapter two—Daniel interpreted the vision of the statue for Nebuchadnezzar in 600 BC. Daniel applied this vision entirely to king Nebuchadnezzar; therefore, we are certain he did not understand the applicability of this vision to the future church. This vision most certainly provided Daniel relief because the interpretation resulted in his life being spared and receiving rewards.

2. Chapter four—Daniel interpreted another dream for Nebuchadnezzar in about 595 BC—a vision of a tree. Daniel writes that this vision caused him grief:

   > Then Daniel (also called Belteshazzar) was greatly perplexed for a time, and his thoughts terrified him. (Daniel 4:19)

   Daniel is distraught because he must give the hotheaded and trigger-happy king bad news; he is a young man who is extremely frightened. Daniel hadn't rebuked the king for erecting an idol based on the vision of the statue, so we know Daniel is timid around Nebuchadnezzar. This vision points directly to Jesus as the tree of life described in the book of Revelation, but Daniel, again as expected, only sees the connection to Nebuchadnezzar's life—he didn't expand on this vision.

3. Chapter five—Daniel interprets writing on the wall during Belshazzar's rule (539 BC) and this vision has no

applicability to the future besides warning rulers and people that should you reject and mock God you will certainly experience death:

> Then Daniel answered the king, "You may keep your gifts for yourself and give your rewards to someone else. Nevertheless, I will read the writing for the king and tell him what it means." (Daniel 5:17)

Daniel is happy that God is planning on removing Belshazzar as the ruler over God's people. Daniel ended this story by saying Belshazzar was killed and Darius the Mede took over, but we know from the rest of the evidence in the book of Daniel that Darius did not rule over Daniel until near the end of his life, therefore, Darius could not have taken over the kingdom. Some of this evidence presented in this section of scripture that Daniel wrote proves that Cyrus the Mede ruled prior to Darius and took over the kingdom at age sixty-two. We will present that later in this book.

4. Chapter six—Daniel is thrown into the den of lions (522 BC):

> So Daniel prospered during the reign of Darius and the reign of Cyrus the Persian. (Daniel 6:28)

Daniel prospered during the reign of these kings because they followed the Lord. Daniel presents this story next because Daniel has already been presented a very basic vision of the future of the church (the vision of the statue

in 600 BC) and the coming of the Messiah (the vision of the tree in 595 BC) which, by the time he assembled his book, he likely understood. Through this event, Daniel wants you to know that God made unbreakable promises to his people that would be fulfilled. Daniel injected the story here about how his life was spared even though he had received a death sentence. Sound familiar? Isn't that what Jesus did for us? Also, in this story, Daniel focuses on the unbreakable decree of the Medes and Persians. The law of the Medes and Persians, once written, is permanent and cannot be repealed. Again, does this sound like God's promise for redemption through a future Messiah—Jesus? You bet—what Daniel wrote provided the decree of the seventy sevens that prophesized this!

5. Chapter seven—In chapter six, Daniel described an event from 522 BC, but now he will go back in history to present a vision he received in 541 BC when Belshazzar was ruler. Daniel witnesses a brief overview of the future of God's kingdom on earth with a focus on a beast who will corrupt and take over the church. However, at the end of this vision, Daniel is told that the Messiah rules over the kingdom of God and the people of God will be redeemed into the presence of God:

> I, Daniel, was troubled in spirit, and the visions that passed through my mind disturbed me. (Daniel 7:15)

> This is the end of the matter. I, Daniel, was deeply troubled by my thoughts, and my face turned

pale, but I kept the matter to myself. (Daniel 7:28)

Daniel is deeply troubled by this vision because he doesn't understand the message. Daniel didn't understand the meaning of this vision until he put his book together because he inserted this vision *after* an explanation of God's decree for the Messiah, but *prior* to the vision that provided vivid details of the decree (chapter nine).

6. Chapter eight—Daniel presents the second vision he received near the end of Belshazzar's reign in 539 BC that describes the entire future of the covenants—the ram and the goat:

I was appalled by the vision; it was beyond understanding. (Daniel 8:27)

I, Daniel, was worn out, and lay exhausted for several days. (Daniel 9:27)

Daniel is again provided a very brief vision of the future of God's kingdom on earth—the church. There will be a power struggle between good and evil and, for a time, evil will prevail. However, like the previous vision, the last verse presents the kingdom of God returning to God forever, and this is a good story. This vision differs from the previous vision because it provides a very specific description of the time of the end. Daniel again did not understand this vision when he received it, but he certainly understood it when he assembled his book because

he placed this vision with the general details of the time
of the Messiah after the first related vision, but prior to
the specific Messiah details presented in the next vision.

7. Chapter nine—In 522 BC, Daniel received the vision
that together with the message he obtained from being
thrown into the lion's den, allowed him to finally understand his visions. Daniel has been telling us all along in
his visions that he is distraught, troubled, and does not
understand what the Holy Spirit is trying to tell him.
Does this sound like my experience with visions? With
this vision, Daniel finally understands that the Lord had
fulfilled Jeremiah's promise right on schedule in 535
BC with a description of the permanent redemption of
God's people, but Daniel didn't understand this message
at the time of this vision. Prior to receiving this vision,
Daniel was "distraught." After this vision and the lion's
den event, Daniel was able to assemble his book—Daniel
makes no negative comments such as being "appalled"
by this vision or it being "beyond understanding."

8. Chapters ten through twelve—In 535 BC, seventy years
after the seventy-year promise of redemption for the
people of God made to Jeremiah, Daniel received a vision that fulfilled that prophecy:

At that time, I, Daniel, mourned for three weeks.
(Daniel 10:2)

I heard but did not understand. So I asked, "My
lord, what will the outcome of all this be? He re-
plied, "Go your way, Daniel, because the words

44

are rolled up and sealed, until the time of the end." (Daniel 12:9)

Daniel is mourning prior to receiving this vision in 535 BC because he was expecting to see Israel redeemed according to Jeremiah's prophecy. At the end of this vision, Daniel admits he doesn't understand, but the angel Gabriel delivering this vision promises Daniel that when his death has arrived (until the time of the end), the vision will be unraveled and he will understand this vision, and in fact the entire message the Holy Spirit provided him throughout his life. The prophecy that Daniel would eventually understand prior to his death was fulfilled in 522 BC with Daniel's last vision of the Messiah and the experience of eternal life through the unbreakable decree God made with his people.

I have presented just a brief snapshot trying to explain to you Daniel's lack of understanding of his visions and the Holy Spirit helping him out. Daniel did not understand his visions until the end of his life in 522 BC, but this is no surprise as he was told in a vision in 535 BC that the visions he had received would be sealed until his time of the end. At the end of Daniel's life in 522 BC, we know that the words were *unsealed*, and Daniel completely understood the meaning of his life. It's a beautiful but complex story that has been put together as directed by the Holy Spirit. I hope you can see how the Holy Spirit provided me my experience of having trouble understanding visions to allow me to peek into Daniel's life and unravel the mystery of the presentation of his book and clear up details of his visions.

One final thought as we close this chapter; my nonbelieving friend has many dreams he relates to events in his life. He is not searching for God in them or searching for God at all. I truly believe that if he searched for God, he would find God in his dreams and would be in awe of the power of the Holy Spirit, just as I am. God proclaimed many years ago that he would provide dreams and visions to people in the future:

> It will happen afterward that I will pour out my Spirit on all flesh; and your sons and your daughters will prophesy. Your old men will dream dreams. Your young men will see visions. (Joel 2:28)

The author of the book of Acts who we determined to be Silas, quoted Peter (Acts 2:16) as telling believers that Joel's prophecy was fulfilled through the coming of the Holy Spirit into the hearts of all peoples of the world and we are still in this time. It is not unusual for people to receive visions or dreams from the Holy Spirit. It is up to you though to search them to find God and start that two-way communication.

We turn now from a general introduction to Daniel to specific concepts that are needed to provide the foundation for our understanding of the book of Daniel.

CHAPTER 4

"Sevens"

A S WE ALREADY DISCUSSED, there are a few important points we need to borrow from the book of Revelation to perform a complete and accurate analysis and interpretation of the book of Daniel. In the last chapter, we found the term *understand* to be a prominent word and an important aspect of the book of Daniel. In Revelation, we find an emphasis on the word *seven*. The site www.biblegateway.com tells us that there are eighty-one references to *seven* in the New Testament and nearly half of these, a total of thirty-six, are presented in Revelation. Although Daniel does not mention *seven* an abnormally high number of times, it has a reference to the most important sevens presented in scripture—the *seventy sevens* of Daniel. Presenting and analyzing the sevens is the first concept we will address because without the meaning of Revelation sevens applied to Daniel, the interpretation of the seventy sevens—the next subject we will address—will not be unraveled. Beware though and buckle up your seatbelt because we are about to take you on an amazing journey through Daniel that makes so much sense you will wonder why it has taken so long for the truth of Daniel to be told.

Without further ado, from Revelation we present a few of the thirty-six references to the number seven:

1. The seven churches (Revelation 1:4)
2. Seven spirits before the throne (Revelation 1:4)
3. Seven golden lampstands (Revelation 1:12)
4. Seven stars (Revelation 1:16)
5. Seven lamps (Revelation 4:5)
6. A scroll with seven seals (Revelation 5:1)
7. Seven horns and seven eyes which are the seven spirits of God (Revelation 5:6)
8. Seven angels with seven trumpets (Revelation 8:2)
9. Seven thunders (Revelation 10:3)
10. Seven signs (Revelation 12:1)
11. Seven crowns (Revelation 12:3)
12. Seven plagues (Revelation 15:6)
13. Seven bowls filled with the wrath of God (Revelation 15:7)
14. Seven hills (Revelation 17:9)
15. Seven kings (Revelation 17:10)

Seven, as it is presented in the book of Revelation, indicates something that is complete and thorough —it cannot be added to or deleted from—it is whole. Revelation 1:4 tells us about the completeness of the trinity of God, who is, was, and always will be together with the Holy Spirit—the seven spirits who, with Jesus, are at the throne of God. In addition, from Revelation 1:20 we learn that the seven churches are also referred to as *"the seven golden lampstands"* because they spread the light of the world, and the seven stars are the angels assigned to watch over the church.

However, I think there is one reference to seven in Revelation that points us directly to Daniel and it is contained in the following verse:

> Then I saw in the right hand of him who sat on the throne a scroll with writing on both sides and sealed with seven seals. (Revelation 5:1)

God is sitting on the throne holding a scroll that has the complete message of the mission of Jesus. And what is this message? God is sending Jesus to earth as the conqueror (Revelation 6:1) who will wage war against the devil and there will be many battles, but in the end Jesus wins! The time of the New Covenant will be the time of Jesus and God provided us all the details of this New Covenant in advance. If we take this meaning from the sevens in Revelation and apply it to Daniel, we can see the prophecy of the seventy sevens in Daniel 9:24–27 as applying only to Jesus.

In the introduction to the book of Revelation, the New International Version (NIV) Study Bible states, "Symbolically, the number seven stands for completeness." As I was editing this section, I was interested to find out whether the NIV Bible explained Daniel 9:24–27 with this same reference because, after all, that prophecy mentions seven sevens and seventy sevens, and that's a lot of sevens. I read the NIV explanation for Daniel 9:24–27 and found that it did not reference the completeness of the seven. To me, this is a complete—pun intended—oversight, and I wondered how anyone could miss this connection when trying to interpret the seventy sevens.

It took me over a year of long days and short-sleep nights to understand the messages in Daniel and Revelation and, at first, I struggled with the meaning of the seventy sevens. After several weeks of prayer, it became the first prophetic puzzle in these two books that the Holy Spirit had me accurately determine. The breakthrough came with the understanding that the seven sevens in that prophecy, as previously stated, not only referred to Jesus—it is Jesus. With that, the meaning of *seventy sevens* unravels as the decree or mandate made by God to predict the most complete event throughout God's creation —the coming of Jesus as the transition from the Old Covenant to the New Covenant.

There are three aspects of the sevens that we need to address in this chapter. First, the seventy sevens is the transition from the Old Covenant to the New Covenant, so we will take you on a very brief journey through scripture to get to this transition. Second, there is a very important piece of the creation story that applies to the seventy sevens that, without the seventy sevens, remains an unsolved puzzle. From this understanding, we can completely unwrap the meaning of *seventy sevens* and we will do this for you in the next chapter. Third and finally, there is another important aspect of the sevens buried in the creation story that allows us to unravel a very special portion of scripture that was sealed in the time of Daniel, and seems to have remained sealed until now. This sealed scripture in Daniel 8:14 and 8:26 provides an indication that we are getting near the time of the end. We will address this connection as we close out this chapter.

First, we want to briefly address the aspect of how you will find the seventy sevens of Jesus presented in Daniel to be the transition from the Old Covenant to the New Covenant. In Genesis, we find the beginnings of the *Old Covenant,* an agreement between God and his people, made with a man named Abraham. From https://www.teachbible.org/gods-covenant-abraham/ we have the following summary:

> **Abrahamic Covenant.**
>
> Now I will highlight all eight points of the promise to Abram, which is explained in Genesis 12:1–3. This is what God said to Abram, "Now the Lord said to Abram, "Go forth from your country, and from your relatives and from your father's house, To the land which I will show you; And I will make you a great nation, and I will bless you, and make your name great; and so shall be a blessing; and I will bless those who bless you; and the one who curses you I will curse, and in you all the families of the earth shall be blessed." Now, look at each of these eight promises in detail.
>
> 1. I will show you a land (12:1d)
> 2. I will make you a great nation (12:2a)
> 3. I will bless you (12:2b)
> 4. I will make your name great (12:2c)
> 5. You shall be a blessing (12:2d)
> 6. I will bless those who bless you (12:3a)
> 7. I will curse him who curse you (12:3b)
> 8. In your "seed" all the families of the earth shall be blessed (12:3c)

In this summary taken from Genesis 12:1–3, we find that God promised Abraham that he will make Abraham into a great nation and will bless him. Abraham's descendants will grow into a great blessed nation and the name of Abraham will be great. Most important of all, there is a description of the New Covenant of the Messiah; through a seed of Abraham "all families of the earth shall be blessed." First, Abraham will be a blessing and all who bless Abraham are blessed, too; then, in the future, the blessing of all people will come through another.

God commanded that there will be only one covenant between God and his people; the people of God were not to make covenants with others:

> He said, "Behold, I make a covenant: before all your people I will do marvels, such as have not been worked in all the earth, nor in any nation; and all the people among who you are shall see the work of Yahweh; for it is an awesome thing that I do with you. Observe that which I command you today. Behold, I will drive out before you the Amorite, the Canaanite, the Hittite, the Perizzite, the Hivite, and the Jebusite. Be careful, lest you make a covenant with the inhabitants of the land where you are going, lest it be for a snare among you; but you shall break down their altars, and dash in pieces their pillars and you shall cut down their Asherah poles; for you shall worship no other god; for Yahweh, whose name is Jealous, is a jealous God. (Exodus 34:10–14)

I presented this passage because there is an important term that we find in both books of prophecy, Daniel and Revelation—the *inhabitants of the land*. The "inhabitants of the land" are the same as the *inhabitants of the earth* that you will see referred to in both the books of Daniel 4:35 and Revelation 3:10, 6:10, 8:13, and 13:8. The *inhabitants of the earth* are people who choose to make covenants with others rather than hold to the covenant made with the one true God of heaven. God cautioned people to keep the covenant with him and only him, because making and keeping covenants with others beside the one true God will lead to destruction.

Afterwards, a descendant of Abraham named Moses recorded the law that God provided the people of his covenant to follow—the Ten Commandments (Exodus 20). But the law is not complete; there are ten commandments and not seven. The law is not complete because nobody can completely follow the law. Therefore, there will be an addition to the law later—the Messiah. In the meantime, since nobody can completely follow the law perfectly, God provided a system of worship and sacrifices to atone for sin. Sacrifices will continue to be required from people to have their sins forgiven until the seventy sevens of Daniel is fulfilled with the arrival of the seven sevens—then, the covenant will be complete.

The world was promised a perfect and complete New Covenant through a coming Messiah whereby the sins of people would be permanently washed away through the blood of the sacrifice of the Messiah. Theologians claim there are over 300 prophetic scripture references to the coming of Jesus as the New Covenant. Dated from the first prediction written in Genesis by Moses sometime between 1500 BC and 1400 BC, to

the final prediction written by Malachi in 440/439 BC, many of the Old Testament prophets predicted a changing of the guard in the future—a transition to the New Covenant. You might be scratching your head a bit if you are a scholar of scripture because I just provided an exact year for Malachi's prophecy, and you have never seen this before. The proof of this exact year for Malachi's prophecy will be provided in the next chapter.

The site https://www.newtestamentchristians.com/bible-study-resources/351-old-testament-prophecies-fulfilled-in-jesus-christ/ lists 351 prophecies about the coming Messiah made by numerous prophets. I give the theologian who developed this website kudos for including Daniel 9:24–27 in his list of prophecies that predict the coming of Jesus, because not all do. For example, the site https://www.learnreligions.com/prophecies-of-jesus-fulfilled-700159 lists forty-seven messianic predictions including two from the book of Daniel (2:44 and 7:13–14) but neglects to include in this list what is the most complete prophecy of the Messiah ever made, Daniel 9:24–27. Can you imagine leaving off the scripture God told us was most important?

Continuing with our discussion of the transition between the covenants, examples of the promise of this transition from the Old Covenant to the New Covenant are provided by God in the following scripture:

> And I will put enmity between you and the woman, and between your offspring and hers; he will crush your head, and you will strike his heel. (Genesis 3:15)

Another, written by Jeremiah, provides more details:

> "The days are coming," declares the Lord, "when
> I will make a new covenant with the people of
> Israel and with the people of Judah. It will not
> be like the covenant I made with their ances-
> tors when I took them by the hand to lead them
> out of Egypt, because they broke my covenant,
> though I was a husband to them," declares the
> Lord. "This is the covenant I will make with the
> people of Israel after that time," declares the
> Lord. "I will put my law in their minds and write
> it on their hearts, I will be their God, and they
> will be my people. No longer will they teach their
> neighbor, or say to one another 'Know the Lord,'
> because they will all know me, from the least of
> them to the greatest," declares the Lord. "For I
> will forgive their wickedness and will remember
> their sins no more." (Jeremiah 31:31–34)

Unlike the terms of the first covenant, when the Messiah arrives with the second covenant *all* people will have the opportunity to know God and follow his ways for eternal life (I will
put my law in their minds and on their hearts). There will come
a time when *all* "the people of Israel," the people of God, know
the laws of God because it will be written "on their heart." The
new covenant with Jesus will include the permanent forgiveness of the sins of the people of God (I will forgive their wickedness and will remember their sins no more). Jesus explained
how this is done—believe in him and your sins are forgiven.

The transition from the Old Covenant to the New Covenant will be through Jesus and, as you will see in the following chapters, the complete details of this transition are provided in the seventy sevens of Daniel.

Next, we turn to the story of creation to point out a very important detail that will help unravel the seventy sevens. We find it in Genesis at the beginning of creation:

> Then God said, "Let us make man in our image, according to our likeness; let them have dominion over the fish of the sea, over the birds of the air, and over the cattle, over all the earth and over every creeping thing that creeps on the earth. So God created man in His own image; in the image of God He created him; male and female He created them. (Genesis 1:26–27)

Note that the term *us* is used for God as the creator rather than the singular term *I*. This is a clear and intentional reference to the trinity of God—God, Jesus, and the Holy Spirit, who have all existed forever and together comprise the entity we call "God." The trinity of God has existed forever and in unity they created everything. All three are equally and independently God—the creator of all things. This means that Jesus *was* from the beginning and *will* be for all times. File this fact away for the next chapter because Jesus is a very important aspect of the seventy sevens called the "seven sevens."

Now, for the third and final point we need to make prior to getting into the details of the seventy sevens, we continue in the story of creation. God tells us that we are to understand that the process of creation was completed in seven days, and it was good. However, there is a big difference between the first six days of creation and the seventh day presented—nothing was created on the seventh day because it was a day of rest. We find then that God created the world in *six* days, but Revelation seems to be telling us that only a seven is complete. Let's take a close look at creation to see if we can find an answer to this dilemma.

We find the description of creation presented in the book of Genesis from the World English Bible (WEB) translation to specify that *all* of creation is put in terms of one specific phrase:

- The first day of creation God created the day and the night—Genesis 1:3–5: "There was evening and there was morning, the first day."
- The second day of creation God separated the water from the sky—Genesis 1:6–8: "There was evening and there was morning, a second day."
- The third day of creation God separated the land, where he grew vegetation, from the sea—Genesis 1:9–13: "There was evening and there was morning, a third day."
- The fourth day God created the stars, sun, and the moon—Genesis 1:14–19: "There was evening and there was morning, a fourth day."
- The fifth day God created the birds and sea life—Genesis 1:20–23: "There was evening and there was morning, a fifth day."
- The sixth day God created mankind, animals, and land life—Genesis 1:24–31: "There was evening and there was morning, a sixth day."

- The seventh day—God rested.

We have six days of creation in terms of "evenings and mornings" then there is that day of rest. As stated, since we know from Revelation that a seven is complete, we can make an argument that creation was not yet complete because there were only *six* references to the "evenings and mornings." One more reference is needed for creation to say it has been completed.

If it feels like there is more to the creation story, you are following along with me. I searched for those special words of creation, *evenings and mornings,* and found only two more additional references to it in all of scripture—and both just happen to be found in the book of Daniel. From the WEB because we want to be consistent with our terminology using the same interpretation, we obtain the following from Daniel:

> He said to me, "To two thousand and three hundred evenings and mornings. Then the sanctuary will be cleansed." (Daniel 8:14)

> "The vision of the evenings and mornings which has been told is true; but seal up the vision, for it belongs to many days to come." (Daniel 8:26)

Verse 8:14 explains the "evenings and mornings" statement and verse 8:26 confirms it as a true event that "belongs to many days to come." Both these verses reference the same thing, and it appears to be something very important because Daniel is told to seal up the vision. This alone is an important fact because in Daniel 12:9, the messenger told Daniel that "the words are rolled up and sealed, until the time of the end," indicating that Daniel would not understand the message he was being shown until he was about to die. In Daniel 8:26, the words are sealed up and we are told the reason for it, "for it belongs to many days to come"; but, Daniel is never told *when* this prophecy will be unsealed and understood.

We do know that this prophecy addresses a long time to come (many days) and belongs to something; but, what is that something? I believe the reference "to many days to come" is the connection to the time of God's creation—the finality of creation—the duration. With the seventh mention of "evenings and mornings" presented in Daniel, creation will be complete— it will end. How do we know? I hate to leave you hanging, but you'll have to take my word for it until we get to the analysis of Daniel 8:14 a bit later in this book. When we get to chapter eight of Daniel you will see how the verses leading up to Daniel 8:14 indicate that this verse is describing the time of the end. I apologize for leaving you hanging a few times in this chapter, otherwise I'd be taking numerous sidebars and lose my place and lose you too!

We have addressed all three aspects of the sevens that we set out to complete in this chapter, so now we turn to the analysis of the seventy sevens, and this will take two chapters to complete.

CHAPTER 5

Seventy "Sevens"—It's All about Jesus

*T*ITLED THIS CHAPTER IN response to the many misinterpretations that have missed the mark for these very special verses presented in Daniel 9:24–27. I'm making a blunt statement in the title as it should be—the seventy sevens is all about Jesus! The prophecy of the seventy sevens given to Daniel is the official transition from the Old Covenant of animal sacrifices to the one-time sacrifice of the Messiah that will start the New Covenant, and it is all about Jesus. There is nothing in the seventy sevens that point to a mysterious tribulation, a coming antichrist, or rapture—it's all Jesus!

I don't like to dwell on past interpretations that contradict what we find, but I will say a few words about this prophecy because it is so important. The misinterpretation of these verses is the single biggest error made by theologians who do not seem to have had a great track record for telling the world the meaning of prophetic scripture written in Daniel or Revelation. For example, https://www.compellingtruth.org/seventy-sevens.html provides the following summary that is typical of most I have read and heard in discussions and pastor sermons:

In summary, the seventy sevens refers to 490 years, 483 of which have been fulfilled, with a future seven-year period of prophecy yet to take place in the future. We believe this will occur after the rapture during the seven-year tribulation described in Revelation.

Where is Jesus in this interpretation? If you continue reading, you might find Jesus somewhere in the calculations made to fit 483 years, but I'm not sure about finding Jesus in the mysterious other seven years explained by a tribulation and rapture story. Many years ago, I took a close look at the theory of the coming tribulation, antichrist, tribulation, and rapture and couldn't make heads or tails of it. I tried to connect the theory to scripture but repeatedly failed to see the connection.

We will start to tear apart the stories of tradition embedded in the interpretations of prophecy in the remainder of this chapter, then will completely break it up when you see how beautiful and complete the prophecy is by describing the coming of Jesus and his completed mission. But enough time spent on theories that don't make sense, let's get to the correct analysis and determination of the meaning of the *seventy sevens*. Repeated for emphasis, a "seven" indicates completeness therefore "seven sevens" *must refer* to Jesus, the epitome of completeness—the origin of the New Covenant. Furthermore, a decree of "seventy sevens" is a reference to the most important and complete permanent promises ever written. What else could it be besides a reference to the coming of Jesus—the Son of God? Since I knew with certainty that the seventy sevens was all about Jesus, solving it became a puzzle with a math problem embedded in it. My initial task of understanding the prophecy in Daniel was based on figuring out God's math problem presented to the world in those four verses, Daniel 9:24–27.

It took several weeks of detailed praying and direction from the Holy Spirit for the flash of light to hit my brain and tell me that we had solved it. I still recall how afterward I offered thanks to God and praised him for revealing the solution to me! Knowing that many had tried and failed to resolve this mystery, solving the math and puzzle problem left me in awe of what God had revealed to me.

We start our analysis of these four verses by finding that Daniel received and documented the overall scope of the message of this vision:

> Seventy "sevens" are decreed for your people and your holy city to finish transgression, to put an end to sin, to atone for wickedness, to bring in everlasting righteousness, to seal up vision and prophecy and to anoint the Most Holy Place. (Daniel 9:24)

Wow, there's a lot in that one verse. We find that this wonderful and permanent declaration was provided by God to declare (Seventy "sevens" are decreed) how the people of God (your people) will connect with God (your holy city). This mandate, as we already stated, is the means to bridge the gap between a perfect God and an imperfect sinning creation. This event being declared and described will end sin (finish transgression, to put an end to sin), therefore, it will remove the requirement of animal sacrifice. This does not mean that God

is forgetting sin, he will permanently *forgive sin* (to atone for wickedness) and that is a huge difference. God does not forget sin unless it is forgiven!

The seventy sevens will at some point allow people in the future to be considered holy enough to forever be in the presence of God (everlasting righteousness). The effects of the seventy sevens will not change over time or ever. The seventy sevens will be a time when visions and prophecy end (to seal up vision and prophecy) and when the Messiah arrives (and to anoint the Most Holy Place). Once the Messiah arrives, nothing more is needed for salvation. The Messiah will come to *free* the world of sin! Hallelujah!

Verse 9:24 ended with a reference to the *"Most Holy Place,"* so let's look at the meaning of this in the following scripture to ensure we captured the interpretation correctly:

> Set up the tabernacle according to the plan shown you on the mountain. Make a curtain of blue, purple, and scarlet yarn and finely twisted linen, with cherubim woven into it by a skilled worker. Hang it with gold hooks on four posts of acacia wood overlaid with gold and standing on four silver bases. Hang the curtain from the clasps and place the ark of the covenant law behind the curtain. The curtain will separate the Holy Place from the Most Holy Place. Put the atonement cover on the ark of the covenant law in the Most Holy Place. Place the table outside the curtain on the north side of the tabernacle

and put the lampstand opposite it on the south side. (Exodus 26:30–35)

It is clear from the book of Exodus that the *Holy Place* is the temple of God, and the *Most Holy Place* is where the law of God resided. Daniel 9:24 tells us that the seventy sevens will provide the details of what will happen "to anoint the Most Holy Place." The seventy sevens will culminate with the designation of a new place of worship now called a "church" that will be anointed with the Messiah. Jesus confirms that he did not come to remove the law from the Most Holy Place:

> Do not think that I have come to abolish the Law or the Prophets; I have not come to abolish them but to fulfill them. (Matthew 5:17)

Jesus stated that he did not come to replace the law, he came to fulfill it. Just as proclaimed in Daniel 9:24, Jesus would be combined with the law of God to provide the New Covenant— he would be anointed as the new path to becoming right with God. Together with Jesus, the seven sevens, the law becomes complete.

The next verse starts to provide details of the seventy sevens and with that comes the period of silence in prophecy (seal up visions and prophecy) that was introduced in Daniel 9:24 (to seal up vision and prophecy):

> Know and understand this; From the time the word goes out to restore and rebuild Jerusalem until the Anointed One, the ruler comes, there will be seven "sevens," and sixty-two "sevens."

It will be rebuilt with streets and a trench, but in times of trouble. (Daniel 9:25)

First, Daniel is told to pay special attention to this prophecy (Know and understand this) so it must be very important and the Lord wants to ensure that Daniel "gets it." As we discussed earlier, there is no doubt that Daniel was having trouble understanding what message the Lord had been providing him throughout his lifetime of visions and interpretations, but this is the key to that very important prophecy of Daniel. With this statement, the Lord wanted to ensure that Daniel would study the meaning of this very carefully so that he would understand. This was the vision that would open Daniel's eyes to understand his lifetime of visions and interpretations. Suddenly, Daniel will see everything as though a flash of light went off in his head—that is my cheap description of Daniel from what I have experienced.

In verse 9:25, we have two *date* points referenced; the first date point is "from the time the word goes out to restore and rebuild Jerusalem," and the second is "until the Anointed One, the ruler comes." The first event mentioned is a prophecy (the word goes out) about the coming Messiah (restore and rebuild Jerusalem). The second event is the arrival time of the coming Messiah (the Anointed One, the ruler comes). It makes complete sense that these two events are related and, in fact, specify the same event—the birth of Christ. In conclusion, we are looking for the last prophecy that predicts the coming of Jesus; then, after the prophecy is made, as stated in Daniel 9:24, prophecy will go silent (to seal up vision and prophecy). Afterward, we will look for the arrival of the Messiah.

I searched for the final prophecy that predicted the arrival of the Messiah and found it in the book of Malachi, where this prophet wrote:

> "Behold, I send my messenger, and he will prepare the way before me; and the Lord, whom you seek, will suddenly come to his temple; and the messenger of the covenant, whom you desire, behold, he comes!" says Yahweh of hosts. "But who can endure the day of his coming? And who will stand when he appears? For he is like a refiner's fire, and like launderer's soap; (Malachi 3:1–2)

It's obvious that Malachi has predicted the coming of John the Baptist (Behold, I send my messenger, and he will prepare the way before me) and the promised Messiah (and the Lord, who you seek, will suddenly come). The next part of this scripture verifies that Jesus is the owner of the temple; it is *his* church (*his* temple). This is not just *a* temple it is *Jesus'* temple. The Messiah will come to the church that he owns, and he will replace the Old Covenant made with Abraham with his New Covenant (the messenger of the covenant, whom you desire). The Messiah, as the replacement for the sacrifice, will forgive the sins of people (he is like a refiner's fire) and purify them (like launderer's soap).

Malachi's prophecy, the last one of the Old Testament prophets who predicted the coming of the Messiah, fulfills the scripture from Daniel 9:25 (From the time the word goes out to restore and rebuild Jerusalem). Jesus is the *new* Jerusalem—the

place where people will go to find God. If you question that, research how many times in scripture people are told to follow Jesus and *come* to him for salvation. People used to go to the temple in Jerusalem and after Jesus arrives, they will go to Him.

Prophecy went silent after the words of Malachi were documented. Daniel 9:25 tells us that in between that last prophecy and the time of the coming of the Messiah, there will be *"seven 'sevens,' and sixty-two 'sevens.'"* The million-dollar question is what are these two things? We already stated earlier that the seven "sevens" was a reference to Jesus; but wait, if this is so, prophecy claimed that Jesus existed prior to his coming to earth as a man. Remember that scripture from Genesis 1:26–27 I asked you to file because we would refer to it—the mention of the trinity? We are here—Jesus existed prior to his coming to earth as a man. Jesus was from the beginning and always was, therefore, the seven "sevens" in that prophecy has just been verified. Jesus existed *prior* to his coming to earth and, therefore, the seven "sevens" of Daniel 9:25 *was* fulfilled. But you really didn't need the reference to that scripture from Genesis because you already knew this as an accepted fact—the greatest thing that ever existed, Jesus, was up in heaven then was sent to earth in the form of a man, to be the sacrifice to end all sacrifices to God. Scripture proves it time and time again, for example, look at John 1:1, 3:13, and 4:26 and Revelation 1:17.

We have just solved the first part of that prophecy, the "seven sevens," but what about the "sixty-two sevens?" Daniel told us that there will also be sixty-two sevens from the last prophecy, which we know as Malachi 3:1–2, until the Messiah comes. This is certainly where we'll need to get into a bit of math. The NIV provides the following introduction for the book of Malachi:

The similarity between the sins denounced in Nehemiah and those denounced in Malachi suggests that the two leaders were contemporaries. Malachi may have been written after Nehemiah returned to Persia in 433 BC or during his second period as governor. . . . Malachi was most likely the last prophet of the OT era (though some place Joel later).

Malachi provided the last prophecy in the Old Testament, then there were no more prophets, visions, and prophecy pointing to the Messiah—prophecy and visions were sealed up with his final prophecy. The NIV states that Malachi's prophecy was estimated to have been made *after* 433 BC.

Sixty-two sevens cannot mean *weeks* because we know that Jesus came many weeks after 433 BC. Therefore, if a seven can be considered "seven years" we are looking for 434 years (62 sevens x 7 years/seven = 434 years). The NIV and many sources claim that Jesus was born in 5/6 BC, so simple math tells us that if we use the estimate for the birth of Jesus in say 6 BC and subtract the year of Jesus' birth, we end up with the year that Malachi documented this prophecy to be 440 BC (440 BC = 6 BC - 434 years). Is this a possibility?

Various sources estimate that the prophecy in the book of Malachi could have originated anytime between 400 BC through 500 BC or even close to 600 BC. Type the year 440 BC into an internet search for Malachi and you will find several sources referring to this as the possible exact year that Malachi documented the last prediction of the Messiah. As for us, we know that prophecy is exact therefore we can confidently claim that

Malachi wrote this prophecy in 439/440 BC; exactly 434 years or "sixty-two sevens" before Jesus was born. After Malachi's prophecy of Jesus was made in 439/440 BC *all* prophecy was sealed up. We have verification of both portions of that prophecy in Daniel 9:25, but we haven't yet addressed the last few words of that verse. We know that the path to God will be different after the arrival of the Messiah (It will be rebuilt with streets and a trench) and we also know from recorded history that the coming of Jesus will not usher in a time of peace (but in times of trouble). With this, the full meaning of verses 9:24–25 has been completely determined.

We move on to the next verse that provides more details of the time after the sixty-two "sevens" that tell us about the mission of Jesus:

> After the sixty-two "sevens," the Anointed One will be put to death and will have nothing. The people of the ruler who will come will destroy the city and the sanctuary. The end will come like a flood. War will continue until the end, and desolations have been decreed. (Daniel 9:26)

Sometime after the Messiah arrives (After the sixty-two "sevens"), the Messiah will be executed (the Anointed One will be put to death) with no possessions; not even clothes (and will have nothing). Jesus will not die a natural death—he will be killed—and when he is killed, he will have no possessions. How's that for an accurate prediction of the crucifixion of Jesus and the splitting up of his outer garments upon his death? No surprises here because scripture verifies it.

Next, Daniel receives a glimpse into the future. Not only will Jesus be executed, but Daniel is told that the "people of the ruler will come and destroy the city." The Jews will not accept Jesus as the sacrifice that replaces the Old Testament sanctuary and sacrifices, so the religious leaders and their followers will team with the ruling government to destroy Jesus and his legacy which is the church started by the apostles after Jesus returned to heaven as documented in his ascension. The attacks on Jesus and his church will be violent, fast, and devastating (The end will come like a flood).

As you will see prophesized extensively in Daniel and Revelation, the religious leaders and most Jews will not accept Jesus and so they will fight against the Apostolic Church (APC) started by the apostles. The battle between the followers of Jesus in the APC and those out to destroy it will never end (War will continue until the end); engrain this important detail into your brain as we proceed —the church will be corrupted from the beginning until the end. As determined in advance by God, the religious leaders will vacate the new temple of Jesus (desolations have been decreed). The fact that Jesus is the replacement sacrifice will be devastating to the Jews and their followers and will be considered an abomination that will cause them to evacuate the church. The Jews and their followers will evacuate the new church and will persecute anyone who does not follow their false teachers. As decreed, people will reject Jesus and persecute the APC until the end. I hope you are starting to recognize history that verifies this! My last book *The Early Church Father Catholic Fraud* detailed the attacks on the APC by the entity we now know as the RCC. The APC was attacked from the beginning and is still being attacked today.

We have one more verse and it is full of treasure as we wrap up the details of the seventy sevens:

> He will confirm a covenant with many for one seven. In the middle of the "seven" he will put an end to sacrifice and offering. And at the temple he will set up an abomination that causes desolation, until the end that is decreed is poured out from him. (Daniel 9:27)

We just had a brief introduction to the entire future of the church of Jesus Christ and now, in verse 9:27, we are back to the beginning. This one verse provides us the details of what the Messiah will do when he comes to earth in the form of a man. Jesus will "confirm a covenant with many for seven years." In the middle of his "seven," he will be executed as the final sacrifice ever needed for the forgiveness of sin (In the middle of the "seven" he will put an end to sacrifice and offering). The Messiah is prophesized to replace the Old Covenant sacrifice requirements by becoming the sacrifice in the middle of his seven-year mission.

This last verse at first glance seems like it falls off the cliff because it claims that Jesus had a "seven"-year mission because everyone knows and accepts the mission of Jesus to have been three-and-a-half years starting in AD 26 and ending with his execution in AD 30. I will say though that even if it initially seems to contradict history, a "seven" for Jesus' mission would indicate that it is complete! I think this is the verse that some believe refers to the distant future time of the antichrist, tribulation, and rapture that theologians created and proliferated throughout the church. This theory started because theologians did not look hard enough to find Jesus in this scripture; Jesus as the sole reason for the seventy sevens! Imagine trying to explain a prophecy predicting the mission of the Messiah by pointing it to the coming of an antichrist. Can you be any more wrong than that?

In closing this chapter, the sacrifice we know as the crucifixion of Jesus is said to occur "in the middle of the seven," but it does not say *exactly* in the middle. This is an important detail because when we evaluate the additional prophecy in Daniel and Revelation, we find that together they provide the exact timing of the execution of Jesus, and it *does not occur exactly* in the middle of the seven. The next phrase is very important too because it verifies that Jesus will be the abomination of desolation referred to in scripture (Daniel 12:11, Matthew 24:15, Mark 13:14). The presence of Jesus at the altar in the temple or church will cause many people to desert the new church. People will not be able to accept the concept of Jesus being the sacrifice as stated earlier by Malachi (But who can endure the day of his coming?). Jesus, by his sacrifice, will replace the altar sacrifice, and this act will cleanse all people of their sin (For he is like a refiner's fire, and like launderer's soap).

There is no doubt that throughout history there has been only one who fulfilled this prophecy and that is Jesus. The coming of Jesus to earth to start his church was an incredible event never to be repeated, and we know it did not usher in a time of peace—it ushered in "times of trouble" as stated in Daniel 9:25. The Jews hated Jesus and they did not accept him as the replacement of the temple sacrifice. The religious leaders and everyone who followed them abandoned the New Covenant

church and faith. The whole New Testament along with history confirm this prophecy as being fulfilled. False teachers were so intent on removing Jesus from the church they used force and persecution of followers of Jesus to replace him with themselves—history proved this was done by the RCC against the APC. False teachers changed the Word of God, claimed to be from God, then persecuted and executed those who opposed their deity and forced takeover of the APC.

There are no other words to describe this prophecy of the seventy "sevens" other than, "God you are so awesome." I say that because you have just seen how God predicted the exact year of the coming of his son to earth, and in the next chapter you will find out how God gave us the keys through Daniel to unlock Jesus' mission—but only with the help of a later prophecy provided to John the Apostle. God so accurately predicted the coming of Jesus and his mission that I had goose bumps all over my body when the accurate interpretation came to me. We are nowhere close to being through yet because with additional help from the book of Revelation, we are about to completely unravel the seven of Jesus for you and show you how God provided us the breadcrumbs to know that he is awesome, powerful, and all-knowing because he told the world about the future and we can now look back and see the fulfillment of God's predictions and promises.

We move on now to the "seven" of Jesus. . . .

CHAPTER 6

"Seven" of Jesus

*W*E PROVIDED A FEW intricate details of the "seven" of Jesus from Daniel 9:27 earlier. For example, we know that Jesus will be executed in the middle of the seven thereby splitting this seven-year period of Jesus into two parts that may or may not be equal (In the middle of the "seven" he will put an end to sacrifice and offering). I quickly determine that, as my first step to start the analysis of the seven of Jesus, we should assume that the sacrifice is in the middle of the seven and, therefore, there were two equal halves of the seven consisting of 1,277.5 days each. Why this many days? Because seven years with 365 days each is 2,555 days (7 x 365 days/year = 2,555 days) and, since Daniel 9:27 tells us that the seven years will be split by the "sacrifice in the middle of the seven," 2,555 days divided into two equal parts is 1,277.5 days (2,555 days ÷ 2 halves). Based on this result we will search Daniel and Revelation for numbers that are close to 1,277 days. We remember that the sacrifice does not necessarily have to be exactly in the middle at the 1,277.5 days mark, but it could be; therefore, the numbers we search for do not have to be exactly 1,277.5 but they should be close.

Through our search we find the numbers 1,290, and 1,335 presented in the book of Daniel and 1,260 presented twice in the book of Revelation, and all three of these numbers meet the criteria. There was another number presented in Daniel, 2,300

in verse 8:14, and we have already hinted at the meaning of this but have not yet conclusively analyzed it. We will address 2,300 in the next chapter; but for now, Daniel 8:14 does not meet our criteria here so we set it aside. I spent numerous days pondering and trying to solve the "seven" of Jesus with those numbers and, after several weeks of getting nowhere, I felt like my head was going to explode. I had complete confidence that I had a grasp on the meaning of the seventy sevens, but the words *"He will confirm a covenant with many for one seven"* still puzzled me.

As already stated, many resources claim that the mission of Jesus lasted about three-and-a-half years long. In apparent confirmation of this, the NIV provides a duration of Jesus' mission from his baptism in AD 26 to his crucifixion in AD 30, which is about three-and-a-half years. Some simple math told me that the number 1,260 from Revelation might apply. If you look at three-and-a-half years as forty-two months with each month having thirty days in it, three-and-a-half years becomes 1,260 days (42 months x 30 days/month = 1,260 days). This could resolve the first half of the mission of Jesus, but does it?

I turned to the passages in Revelation with the number 1,260 in them and tried to put them into context to see if it was a match:

> The woman fled into the wilderness to a place prepared for her by God, where she might be taken care of for 1,260 days. (Revelation 12:6)

Now I was really baffled. We had a woman fleeing to a place in the wilderness, and what does this have to do with Jesus? First, I had a complicated math problem and now, to add to it,

I have a mystery of a woman to solve. I tried to overcome my frustration as I struggled with it again for several more weeks during which I could only find slivers of progress. Then, I turned to prayer. I guess, like most humans, I want to do everything on my own accord; then, and only then, do I turn to prayer. Once I've exhausted all my options and feel like I've hit the dead end—then, I turn to prayer. We wait because it's human nature to try to do things on our own, but God wants us to turn to prayer first!

In response to my prayer, I received the following vision that I wrote down:

> July 23, 2022—In my vision this morning, I am relearning calculus for some reason. After some thought, I realized the Holy Spirit is prompting me to go over prophecy numbers again and keep analyzing them because they will eventually make sense.

This may not seem like help, but it was all the help I needed—the Holy Spirit addressed my concern and gave me the answer I needed. I'm going to have to take a bit of a sidebar here to do some explaining because you are likely scratching your head trying to determine the connection.

I learned calculus many years ago in college, but it wasn't easy. This was surprising for me because I quickly understood math and was a wiz at the manipulation of numbers. Math was a puzzle and a game to me, and I enjoyed playing with numbers in my head. As time went on, I even took elective classes in college in "Imaginary Math" and "Mathematical Modeling for Chemical

Engineers" just for the fun of it. At the risk of sounding like I'm bragging a bit, I averaged a near 100% in my numerous college level math classes. Please understand that I'm not bragging, I'm just letting you know that I'm one of those strange people who enjoys math and the understanding of it comes easy to me. As a side note, there's that word *understanding* again.

I can recall many years ago when I was only about nine or ten years old being at a bowling alley with my father sitting in one of the two seats reserved for the people who scored the games. It wasn't unusual for me to be sitting in the scoring seat as the designated scorekeeper for both teams. I was watching my dad's five-member team and the five members of an opposing team practice to get ready for an evening match. On this day, as the match was beginning to start, I asked for the names of the players on the opposing team then heard someone shout, "That kid ain't scoring! He's too young and how do we know he won't screw it up!" I was a bit nervous at the remark, then one of the members of my dad's team screamed back at him, "Because he's probably better at math than anyone here. You'll see. This kid doesn't make mistakes." I felt the pressure, but I didn't lose my focus on the job at hand. I finished the three-game team match without making an error; then, as the guy on the other team who made the comment was getting ready to leave, he turned around and apologized to me, thanking me for doing such a good job. I think he gave me a couple bucks too—my first paying gig!

Back to my troubles with calculus—I remembered it as though it was yesterday because this is the only time that I can recall a math concept giving me trouble. For the first two days of being introduced to the concept of calculus, I was lost and frustrated—it just wasn't sinking in, and I wasn't used to this. On the third day, as I sat in class, something like a flash hit my brain then suddenly I immediately and completely understood it. I wasn't sure what happened but in that instant calculus became clear. I know what happened now, based on what I have been finding out about the book of truth that details the future, God planted that roadblock to calculus in my brain, then in a flash gave me the understanding of it so I would remember it and capture this story here in this book. God does know everything and wrote the book with all the set times in it, so I know the Holy Spirit was involved in my life at that instant of understanding of calculus.

Returning to the problem I had at hand to solve, the Holy Spirit was clearly telling me that I was getting close and a solution was at hand—I just needed to be patient and continue manipulating the numbers to dig a bit harder to find the solution. That vision renewed my energy, and I became excited about the incredible challenge! I had already been through the numbers numerous times and was starting to get close but some of what I was determining just didn't quite fit together—a few pieces of the puzzle were off. Then, in another flash I remembered the following vision that I had received about three weeks earlier on July 1, 2022:

> I was told in this vision to continue with the book of Revelation but be careful to not skip any verses.

After I had received that vision, I realized that I was in too much of a hurry to complete the review of prophecy, so I

needed to slow down a bit and look closer at each word of scripture. I went back to the book of Revelation and closely studied scripture, addressing the woman that is mentioned with those 1,260 days. As I read about her, I realized that as time went on this woman kept changing. Jesus never changes so the woman couldn't be Jesus. The disciples didn't change so it can't be them either. Furthermore, the message of salvation stays the same and doesn't change but the woman changes. There was only one thing that came to mind that was changing over time and that was the church—we know this from history and prophecy that predicted the changes in the church, so the woman must be the church. At the beginning, the woman or rather the church, starts out pure, but then over time she becomes very corrupt. In a flash I knew that the woman had to be the church!

I then looked at the scripture that stated the woman was taken to the wilderness and protected for 1,260 days. Hmm . . . at the very beginning, Jesus was with the disciples as they set the foundation for the church. Does this sound like Jesus and the disciples were protected during their mission to provide the foundation for the church of Jesus Christ? I was certain we had a match. Jesus and the disciples were protected for 1,260 days while Jesus provided the foundation of the church through his preaching, teaching, and mentoring of the disciples. The mission of Jesus was to start the church and the mission lasted exactly 1,260 days. A quick review of scripture will confirm for you that Jesus and the disciples were protected by God until the time of Jesus' sacrifice arrived. The execution of Jesus had a set time and prior to this time no harm could come to Jesus and his disciples.

We had that portion solved, but there was the other half of the seven that was still a mystery. Continuing to read about the woman, I found another reference to the protection of her in the book of Revelation:

> The woman was given the two wings of a great eagle, so that she might fly to the place prepared for her in the wilderness, where she would be taken care of for a time, times and half a time out of the serpent's reach. (Revelation 12:14)

The woman was pregnant and has now given birth, signifying that those founding the church, Jesus and his disciples, gave birth to the church when Jesus performed his sacrifice. After giving birth to the church, we learn that the woman is protected for "a time, times and half a time." The term *a time, times and half a time* is generally accepted by theologians as being equal to three-and-a-half years. With "a time, times and half a time" proposed by theologians to represent three-and-a-half years, it was a good path to follow the lead that this description could likely be about the second half of the seven of Jesus.

Taken care of means to be protected, therefore, Revelation is telling us that the woman is again being protected for a set time with an estimated duration of three-and-a-half years. The church was born with the sacrifice of Jesus, and now the disciples, who were commissioned by Jesus to start the church, spread his words and made disciples of people (Matthew 28:16–20). This fit the profile, but were they protected for three-and-a-half years while they gave the fledgling church a

solid footing? Let's look deeper into scripture to determine whether it makes sense or not.

In the book of Acts, we read about the stoning of Stephen (Acts 7:54–60) and the NIV and other sources estimate the execution of Stephen to have occurred around AD 35. We won't verify this date, but we do wonder if it wasn't closer to AD 34—three-and-a-half years after the apostles started the church. We obtain the following summary about the effect that the stoning execution of Stephen had on the early church:

> Saul was consenting to his death. A great persecution arose against the assembly which was in Jerusalem in that day. They were all scattered abroad throughout the regions of Judea and Samaria, except for the apostles. But Paul ravaged the assembly, entering into every house and dragged both men and women off to prison. (Acts 8:1–3)

The stoning death of Stephen is the first recorded execution of those starting the church. From these verses in Acts, the stoning death of Stephen marks the beginning of the physical persecution of the church—here called "the assembly." After this execution of Stephen, those starting the church, except for the apostles, scattered. How best to quickly spread the word then to force followers of Jesus to evacuate the area—just saying . . . God had a plan.

Among those leading the persecution was the man Jesus selected to replace Judas as the twelfth disciple—Saul, who would have his name changed to Paul to signify his rebirth as a follower of Jesus who became the greatest missionary ever. Is this another part of God's plan written ahead of time for the church? Of course! The church start-up was protected for three-and-a-half years from physical persecution, then the protection was lifted, and the persecution of the apostles and followers of Jesus picked up further fulfilling Daniel 9:24–27. We know from the book of Acts that James, the brother of John and a disciple of Jesus, was executed (Acts 12:2). We don't have the documentation of other executions, but from what survived history we can be assured that the woman now morphed into the protected three-and-a-half years period of the start-up of the church.

In summary, the process of starting the church started the moment of Jesus' sacrifice; then, for three-and-a-half years, the disciples and those they recruited to help start the church were protected from persecution. The woman we know as the church was protected for 1,260 days as the foundation of the church was set up, then the church was born, and finally the woman was protected for three-and-a-half years to give the church a solid footing to take hold and prevent it from being extinguished. Later, we read how the woman as the church becomes full of corruption:

> Then the angel carried me away in the Spirit into a wilderness. There I saw a woman sitting on a scarlet beast that was covered with blasphemous names and had seven heads and ten horns. The woman was dressed in purple and scarlet, and was glittering with gold, precious stones, and pearls. (Revelation 17:3–4)

A few verses after this, the woman is referred to as the "mother of prostitutes." The mystery of the woman was confirmed, then the pieces of the puzzle came together. The corruption of the church will be described in detail in both Daniel and Revelation as the beasts who work with the devil took complete control over the church.

We're almost through, but not quite yet as we have two more numbers that we need to address that seem very close to the numbers of the three-and-a-half years we were looking for:

> From the time the daily sacrifice is abolished and the abomination that causes desolation is set up, there will be 1,290 days. Blessed is the one who waits for and reaches the 1,335 days. (Daniel 12:11–12)

We know that the daily sacrifice was abolished in AD 30 when Jesus became the sacrifice that replaced the former required temple sacrifices. We also know that Jesus is the abomination that causes desolation; Jesus as the replacement for the temple sacrifices will not be accepted and, therefore, the religious leaders and their followers will vacate the new church. The Jews did not accept the sacrifice of Jesus so from day one they immediately vacated the temple. But read the verse Daniel 12:11 carefully again and you will find two very important words—*set up.*

I reviewed several translations of this verse, and they all contain the same words, *set up.* When I think of something "set up" I think of it as something that is completed. If I have "set up" a process to remove the sacrifice, I have finished the work.

With this in mind, our two data points become the beginning of the start of the church when the sacrifice of Jesus was made in AD 30 (the time the daily sacrifice was abolished) and, although the abomination that causes desolation occurred at the same time, it would not be finished for approximately three-and-a-half years until it is *set up* (and the abomination that causes desolation is set up). The church is under construction until it is completed, then the doors are opened for services. Reading Daniel 12:11, from the time of the sacrifice of Jesus until the setting up of the church is complete, "there will be 1,290 days," therefore, this is a reference to the last half of the seven of Jesus—the persecution of the church will start after those 1,290 days.

We now have both data points for the "seven" of Jesus and both halves are protected periods to allow the church a solid foundation so that it will exist until the eternal church takes its place at the time of the end. We have the mission of Jesus, the "seven" (Daniel 9:27) that lasted 1,260 days (Revelation 12:6) with the sacrifice in the middle (Daniel 9:27), then we have the church being set up (Revelation 12:14) for 1,290 days (Daniel 12:11) until it is commissioned at the end of that time. This is a prime example of how these two prophetic books rely on each other for the complete message!

We started our analysis claiming that the seven-year period will be 2,555 days so these two periods should add up to that number, but we find that they do not. Add the time of the first three-and-a-half-year period (1,260 days) to the time of the second three-and-a-half-year period (1,290 days) and it is very close to the 2,555 days of "seven" years (1,260 days + 1,290 days = 2,550 days), but not exact —it is five days short. We

haven't yet included in our calculation the days required for the sacrifice to be replaced—Jesus being crucified in the middle of the "seven." When we examine the sacrifice of Jesus, we find that it totals five days. The site https://www.biblestudy.org/maps/last-days-of-jesus-timeline.html is a thorough analysis and verifies this length of time, so you can see we are not trying to force fit numbers to make the calculations of the seven of Jesus fit history. You can debate and do your own analysis of these numbers, but if you add the last supper, trial, execution, the days in the grave, and, if you must, add one day for the ascension (only if you have heartburn and your numbers aren't adding up), you will end up with five days total. Adding the time of Jesus' sacrifice (five days) to the days of the mission of Jesus (1,260 days) and to the second half when the disciples are protected to start the church (1,290 days) and you end up with an exact match for the seven of Jesus (2,555 days) specified in Daniel 9:27!

However, we are still not through yet—we have a few more numbers to deal with. First, according to the book of Acts, we know that Jesus made forty days of appearances just after the sacrifice and we haven't yet accounted for these days:

> After his suffering, he presented himself to them and gave many convincing proofs that he was alive. He appeared to them over a period of forty days and spoke about the kingdom of God. (Acts 1:3)

When we look close at these numbers, we find that God did not forget about these forty days—he provided prophetic scripture that predicted and verified that it would happen just as planned. To find the meaning of those 1,335 days of Daniel 12:12 subtract the start-up of the church (1,290 days) and the days of the sacrifice (five days) to get the forty days of appearances (1,335 days − 1,290 days − 5 days = 40 days). In summary then, the 1,335 days are equal to the time for developing the church to spread the Word of God (1,290 days), plus the time of the sacrifice (five days), plus the days of appearances of Jesus (forty days).

Daniel 12:12 told us that anyone waiting for and witnessing these 1,335 days would be blessed. We know of only one group who had the privilege of participating and witnessing all three of these events, and this is the group of disciples. Only the disciples will witness the sacrifice of Jesus, see Jesus during the forty days of appearances documented in Acts 1:3, then be commissioned to start the church (Matthew 28:16–20). Daniel 12:12 is a reference to the disciples of Jesus. Think about it, this verse is 12:12 and there were twelve tribes of Jacob and twelve disciples of Jesus—get it 12:12? Coincidence? You may consider this aspect and say, "Yah, John, but what about Judas? Judas wasn't there to witness Jesus so there were only eleven disciples present." I respond with, "But you forget Paul! Paul witnessed Jesus after he was crucified, and he was commissioned to start the church." I would propose that the disciples might have jumped the gun a bit when they selected the replacement of Judas because it certainly seems like Jesus picked Paul in advance to replace Judas.

As we close this chapter, remember earlier when I noted that Daniel 9:27 told us that the Messiah would replace the sacrifice in the middle of the seven, but it was not stated that it would

be *exactly* in the middle, and I asked you to file that information? The two halves of Jesus mission are close in duration, but they are not exact, and according to prophetic scripture they did not have to be exact. Another point to make is that when you consider the technicality of the details, the forty days of appearance does not add to the three-and-a-half-year mission of Jesus, the replacement of the sacrifice, or the development of the church. In case you are wondering about this, there is a good reason—forty days of appearances were not necessary to prove that Jesus rose from the dead. The forty days of appearances were not added to the "seven" of Jesus because they are for the doubters and not part of the required mission of Jesus. Jesus only needed one appearance for a moment to prove that he was alive, but God gave us forty days of appearances to help the doubters. It is comforting to know about all this extra evidence of the resurrection of Jesus (Acts 1:2–9, 1 Corinthians 15:3–8, and numerous other verses) because it is icing on the cake to help people believe.

This chapter is already long, but I found an interesting passage as I was completing this portion of the review of Daniel that I needed to close out this chapter with. There are some interesting words in that commissioning scripture from the Gospel of Matthew:

> But the eleven disciples went into Galilee, to the mountain where Jesus had sent them. When they saw him, they bowed down to him, but some doubted. Jesus came to them and spoke to them, saying, "All authority has been given to me in heaven and on earth. Go and make disciples

of all nations, baptizing them in the name of the
Father and of the Son and of the Holy Spirit,
reaching them to observe all things that I commanded you. Behold, I am with you always,
even to the end of the age." Amen. (Matthew
28:16–20)

Note that even after everything the disciples had seen,
"some doubted." This surprised me and it probably surprises
you too. We have disciples who were with Jesus for three-and-
a-half years and witnessed his healing and the many things that
he did—even his death and resurrection—but then we are told
that some still doubted. We are told that they all "bowed down"
but God knew that some still doubted, and this should not be
surprising because we know that one of his disciples, Judas
Iscariot, rejected Jesus and turned him over to be executed for
forty pieces of silver. In my humble opinion, there are a few of
the disciples on the edge of Jesus who never became engaged
or close to Jesus and didn't recognize him as the Messiah. We
know from scripture there are a few disciples who, except for
being selected, we don't know anything about, and my humble
conclusion is that Jesus was referring to one or more of these
disciples.

That previous point alone has an important message for all
of us. There were disciples who saw the things that Jesus did
yet they still doubted. Reading this helped me better understand the doubts I had a few years back and had to address. If
those disciples who saw and walked with Jesus doubted, then
those who periodically have doubts should not be too hard on
themselves. But what more could Jesus have done to prove to

those disciples who doubted that he was God? As we complete this chapter, I ask you, "What more could Jesus do to convince you to believe in him?" You have seen how prophecy predicted his coming to the exact year and predicted to the day the mission of Jesus and the start-up of the church—all predicted nearly 600 years in advance. In addition, you have seen how perfectly God wove together two prophetic books to tell you the exact timing of the mission of Jesus and his disciples. If you are still a doubter in Jesus, I ask you the same question—"What more can Jesus do to convince you to believe?"

To wrap up this chapter, we present the following time line of the "seven" of Jesus that will be included in the overall time line presented in the appendices:

AD 26–30	The first half of the "seven: of Jesus—preaching, teaching, and healing for about three-and-a-half years (Daniel 9:24–27). The period of Jesus' mission lasted for exactly 1,260 days and, during this time, Jesus and his disciples were protected from harm (Revelation 12:1–6). Refresh your memory with how many times scripture recorded Jesus and his disciples escaping harm because it wasn't the designated time of the sacrifice (e.g., John 2:4, 7:6, 12:23).
AD 30	The forty days of appearances of Jesus together with the disciples receiving the Holy Spirit (Acts 1:3–7 and Daniel 12:11–12) and the commissioning from Jesus for the disciples to start the church (Matthew 28:16–20).
AD 30–33	Immediately after the church was started up it was infiltrated by false teachers who were intent on destroying Jesus and his church. The "abomination that causes desolation" was a process that started the moment Jesus replaced the sacrifice (Daniel 9:27) and it lasted throughout the three-and-a-half-year commissioning of the church when even some disciples commissioned to start the church doubted (Matthew 28:16–17). The "abomination that causes desolation" was completed at the end of the commissioning of the church (Daniel 12:11).

AD 30–33	The last half of the "seven" of Jesus (Daniel 9:27) began and lasted for 1,290 days (Daniel 9:26–27). The disciples were protected from harm during this time (Revelation 12:9), but the church was infiltrated and attacked (Acts 1:1–6:7).
AD 30–33	The disciples who witnessed the 1,335 days of Jesus were blessed (Daniel 12:12). They witnessed and participated in the five days of the sacrifice (five days), the appearances after he rose from the dead (forty days), and then performed their job to start the church (1,290 days).
AD 33 and on	The church remains infiltrated by false teachers until the end when the eternal church of Jesus Christ will arrive and all those who followed Jesus will be with God for eternity (references and scripture analysis to come).

CHAPTER 7

The "Hour"

W E HAVE NOW COMPLETED our review of the sevens of Revelation and the seventy sevens of Daniel that predicted the transition from the Old Covenant to the New Covenant through Jesus. Our analysis presented in the last chapter matched historical records to prove that God knew the future before it happened. Not only that, God *wanted* us to understand that he knew the future before it would happen so in advance he provided us all the details of the covenants he made with his people. Note that I said *all* the details—this was intentional, because as we continue our review of Daniel with support from the book of Revelation, you will find a *complete* description of the interaction between God and the people he created.

The execution of Jesus ended the Old Covenant by replacing the continuous animal sacrifices with the one-time sacrifice of Jesus. The sacrifice of Jesus started the time of the New Covenant that we know from scripture and is also referred to as the "hour" and the "end times." First, we put the term *hour* in context from looking at the following scripture:

> But the hour comes, and now is, when the true worshippers will worship the Father in spirit and truth, for the Father seeks such to be his worshippers. (John 4:23)

We have the good news that God will put the Holy Spirit in all people to make it easy to find and worship God. No longer will people have to search for God—he will be in the hearts of all. We know from the Gospel of John that Jesus' disciples were the first to receive this gift from God (John 20:22), then on that Pentecost day recorded in scripture (Acts 2:1–4) God provided the Jews who were selected to spread the church, with his Spirit. God assigned Jesus as the center of worship and placed him in the heart of every person who will exist during the New Covenant (John 3:16–21). John refers to this time of the New Covenant as the "hour."

During the hour of the New Covenant those who die in the Lord will attain that eternal peace:

> Most certainly I tell you, the hour comes, and
> now is, when the dead will hear the Son of God's
> voice; and those who hear will live. (John 5:25)

The "hour" of the New Covenant ushered in a new time when those who follow God will hear the voice of Jesus and will live. I'm not sure why there is so much confusion about death among Christians because this seems plain and simple. During the New Covenant (the hour) that started with Jesus (and now is), those who have chosen to follow Jesus will hear his voice when they die and will live (those who hear will live). Jesus is calling out to everyone while they live because he is in your heart, however, only some will hear his voice when they die to be rewarded with eternal life (and those who hear will live).

John also calls the "hour" of the New Covenant the "end times" because the hour of the New Covenant will be the final period on earth:

> Little children, these are the end times, and as you heard that the antichrist is coming, even now many antichrists have arisen. By this we know that it is the final hour. (1 John 2:18)

John tells us that the New Covenant is currently full of people who are the opposite of everything Jesus is (even now many antichrists) but are acting like they are Jesus—even pretending to have come back from the dead like Jesus (have arisen). As predicted in Daniel 9:24–27, the hour of Jesus will not be a time of peace—it will be a time of turmoil caused by corruption in the church. John tells us that there is evil in the church and it will not stop—their movement will grow and continue (the antichrist) throughout the hour (by this we know that it is the final hour).

John continued to provide more details:

> They went out from us, but they didn't belong to us; for if they had belonged to us, they would have continued with us. But they left, that they might be revealed that none of them belong to us. (1 John 2:19)

The people destroying the church are not strangers—they were selected by the disciples to run the church (They went out from us), but those selected were only pretending to follow Jesus and the words of the disciples (but they didn't belong

to us). John also says that it's obvious that, since they aren't following what the disciples are teaching, they are false teachers (that they might be revealed that none of them belong to us). The message for you in here is that if you have teachers and preachers who aren't sticking to the written words of Jesus, they are false teachers, and it is not hidden—it should be obvious because they are not following Jesus through the documentation the apostles put together.

The following references in Revelation provide additional details of the hour of the end times:

- Those who reject Jesus and create a covenant of evil with others will face trial (Revelation 3:10)
- Heaven will be silent for about half of the time of the end times (Revelation 8:1)
- Many will find eternal death (Revelation 9:15)
- It will be an hour of judgement (Revelation 14:7)
- God will allow leaders who follow evil to exist in the church (Revelation 17:12)

You might have glanced over that second bullet wondering what it meant. The reference to this brief time in heaven initially made no sense; but, after determining its meaning, we found it to help unravel the New Covenant of Jesus. We need this information to complete a thorough analysis of Daniel, so we will take the time to describe the meaning of this very short, but powerful verse of scripture. We start by presenting the whole verse:

> When he opened the seventh seal, there
> was silence in heaven for about half an hour.
> (Revelation 8:1)

What a weird thing for God to say, I thought! We presented the passage describing the seven seals of Jesus earlier as a
scroll that has the complete message of the mission of Jesus
(Revelation 5:1). This is a reference to the opening of the last
seal of that scroll, therefore, the message of the mission of Jesus
is being completed. The earlier seals presented Jesus coming to
earth to save, then a spiritual war is prophesized to begin that
will result in the church being overtaken by a corrupt entity
that will reign over the church for many years. The last period
of Jesus addressed the seventh seal and will coincide with an
apparently brief time of "silence in heaven."

You might ask because I did, why "half an hour" and not
just an hour? Furthermore, why *about* half an hour and not just
a *complete* half an hour? Why is God even mentioning the "silence in heaven" because about half an hour doesn't seem like
a long time and why would this be so important anyway? Why,
why, why, I wondered with these questions rattling around
in my head as I pondered the meaning. Putting this verse in
context, we have already seen how the New Covenant of Jesus
is referenced to be an hour, so intuition tells us that we may
have a split in the New Covenant because this verse references
"about half an hour." For several weeks, I pondered the meaning of this verse then with some guidance from the Holy Spirit,
the meaning came to me like looking at a flash card.

There are numerous verses in prophecy that describe heaven
as a very noisy place. Those that lived their lives according to

the Word of God are rewarded with a gift of heaven and heaven is full of multitudes of souls playing instruments and singing praise songs to Jesus. That alone should get you thinking. If you say you want to go to heaven, do you know what you are asking for? Heaven is a place where you will spend all your time for eternity praising Jesus. If you don't want to praise Jesus now while you are living on earth, what would possibly make you think that you would enjoy spending eternity in heaven praising Jesus? If you are an unbeliever and sitting in the stands in a church in silence because you are embarrassed about praising Jesus, you are not going to like being in heaven praising Jesus for eternity. There is no place described in heaven that would allow you to "sit this one out" as though you were avoiding a dance when you are tired of the praising noise.

A period of silence in heaven can only mean one thing—there is no praising going on. Furthermore, since heaven is all about praising Jesus, if there is no praising going on in heaven, Jesus must not be present. Heaven being silent can only mean one thing—it is closed for business—Jesus has left the building! Jesus is, was, and always will be in his residence in heaven—that is except for two instances documented in scripture that tell us Jesus has left heaven. The first time Jesus left heaven was when he came to earth to fulfill his mission from 5/6 BC to AD 30. This period cannot be the time being described in verse 8:1 of Revelation because the years that Jesus spent on the earth *are the reason* for the ongoing praise in heaven. Heaven is noisy with the praising by the multitudes because they are thanking Jesus for his sacrifice. The praising of Jesus in heaven didn't start until *after* he returned to heaven at the time of his ascension. Only *after* the sacrifice of Jesus does heaven get noisy with praises to Jesus!

That leaves us with the only other recorded incidence of Jesus leaving heaven as described in chapter 20 of the book of Revelation:

> Then I saw thrones on which were seated those who had been given authority to judge. And I saw the souls of those who had been beheaded because of their testimony about Jesus and because of the Word of God. They had not worshipped the beast or its image and had not received its mark on their foreheads or their hands. They came to life and reigned with Christ a thousand years. (Revelation 20:4)

At first glance, you might assume that this verse is referring to the reign of Jesus in heaven; but, this doesn't make sense. Why would scripture tell us something that has been ongoing since Jesus returned to heaven? Although this does not say that Jesus left heaven to go to earth to reign, it makes sense that this *must* be the meaning of this scripture because there has been a change. From the book of Acts, we know that Jesus ascended back to heaven after his forty days of appearances *then*, from Revelation, we know that followers of Jesus are beheaded during the reign of the beast. Then, we learn from Revelation that the rulers of the beast will execute the followers of Jesus until a set number of martyrs is killed—144,000. Once the set number of martyrs is reached, the beast will lose its authority to rule and through this verse we read that Jesus will return to earth to

reign over his church. In summary, the end of the reign of the beast will coincide with the set number of followers of Jesus being martyred, then the martyrs "came to life and reigned with Christ a thousand years."

Jesus is prophesized to return to earth for a thousand years and rule with the resurrected souls of those who were beheaded for "their testimony about Jesus." Since this is the only other time that Jesus leaves heaven, this *must be* equal to the reference to *"about half an hour in heaven."* From this, we learn that one thousand years in heaven is equal to "about half an hour in heaven." Wow! Pay close attention to this concept because there is a very powerful message the Lord is trying to give you here that we will explain in the next chapter. Most theologians agree with this explanation that the thousand-year reign of Jesus will be on earth, but this is where we split company. Theologians and preachers teach that we are waiting for the return of Jesus to rule for that one-thousand-year reign, but scripture tells us that we are currently in the thousand-year reign of Jesus.

Let me explain by addressing that last number that we have pointed to as being connected to creation and we keep hinting that it is important, but we haven't yet analyzed it:

> He said to me, "To two thousand and three hundred evenings and mornings. Then the sanctuary will be cleansed." (Daniel 8:14)

Earlier in this book, we stated that creation would not be completed until we come across the seventh reference to "evenings and mornings" and we found it here in this last verse, then in the following verse:

"The vision of the evenings and mornings which
has been told is true; but seal up the vision, for
it belongs to many days to come." (Daniel 8:26)

This scripture states that there will be 2,300 evenings and
mornings until the sanctuary is cleansed. The sanctuary was
made holy by the sacrifice of Jesus, but we just went through a
whole lot of analysis of scripture that proves the sanctuary was
dirty in the time of John and it will remain dirty during the entire hour of the New Covenant until the time of the end of the
end times. We've already mentioned the reign of the beast and
the transition to the reign of Jesus as two portions of the end
times, but during both of these portions the church will be corrupt. The return of Jesus to earth to reign over his church did
not remove the corruption from the church—as John has told
us in his letters and as you will see when we get into a verse-by-
verse analysis of Daniel the chapter after next.

We know from both Daniel and Revelation that the church
will be cleansed *only* when the eternal church replaces the
church on earth. The eternal church will be holy with all of
God's people present and worshipping Jesus (Revelation 21
and 22). Daniel also provided this beautiful picture of the time
of the end with the eternal church in the first vision he interpreted for Nebuchadnezzar (Daniel 2:44). Before we complete
the meaning of Daniel 8:14 and 8:26, I will ask you to consider
the church—Is the church still corrupt? To answer that question, compare the church now to the church as Jesus committed his sacrifice. Compare the current church to the eternal
church. Is the church pure like it once was or like it will be in
the end? Is sexual immorality and sin prevalent in the church?

Is the church everywhere teaching the Jesus of scripture or are there variations of Jesus being taught through the inclusion of tradition? I think you know the answers to these questions and can agree that the church is still full of corruption. There is no doubt that the church immediately became corrupt, and the sanctuary will not be cleansed for 2,300 years when the eternal church arrives.

I hope you have grasped what we've just proven; the hour of the covenant will end 2,300 years after the beginning of the New Covenant that started in AD 30. In other words, the New Covenant has an expiration date of AD 2330 with the seventh "evenings and mornings" of creation. Creation of humans had a beginning and there will be an end. We have already stated that Jesus came to earth to rule for 1,000 years, and since creation will end with the eternal church, we know that Jesus had to have returned already and, in fact, he returned a thousand years prior to the time of the end in AD 2330. This means that Jesus returned to rule over the church in AD 1330 (2,300– 1,000 years). With this interesting fact in mind, I searched the Internet to see if there was an important event that occurred in AD 1330. With a bit of investigating, I determined that 1330 was the year a man named John Wycliffe was born. And what is the significance of John Wycliffe's birth? God designated this man as the person who would free the words of Jesus from the control of the beast.

John Wycliffe fulfilled a set time in history to translate the Bible into the language of the people and this act would take away the total control of the word by the beast – the great false church. During the reign of the RCC from AD 30–1330 the Gospel was not available for people to read, therefore, Jesus was represented by the words of others who chose how to describe him, rather than reading the truth of Jesus from eyewitnesses who recorded his words and the details of his life. From AD 30–1330, people searched for Jesus but couldn't find him in the church. Once John Wycliffe made the words of Jesus available to everyone in the church, it was as though Jesus came back to reign. The Lord designated this time in history for the words of Jesus to be provided to everyone and this would free the word from the control of the beast. After John Wycliffe translated the Bible for all to read, *all* people had access to Jesus—he was back in the church!

In summary, we have a split New Covenant into two portions—the first part considered to be the reign of the beast, then the thousand-year reign of Jesus when Jesus returned to his church. As we go through Daniel and Revelation you will see plenty of evidence that prove the reign of the beast was prophesied and allowed by God, then by God's decree it ended. The book of Daniel addresses the beast but most of the thorough details of the beast are presented in the book of Revelation. At the end of the reign of the RCC, also called "the reign of the beast," Jesus returned to earth to rule over the church in what you will see will be called "a mixed kingdom" (Daniel 2:41). It will not be a pure sanctuary but there will be part of the church that is sincerely following Jesus. From AD 1330–2330, Jesus will reign over the mixed church and many will follow him and be saved. However, as you will learn, many will still be deceived, and the Lord has a plan for these souls that is specified thoroughly in Revelation and other scripture. If we do not address this in this book, we will get to it in the follow-up book covering Revelation.

Finally, we still have neither discussed the term *about half an hour* nor explained what I meant when I stated that there is a powerful message from God in that snippet of scripture. This chapter is already getting long, so we will address these two aspects of Revelation 8:1 in the next chapter. But first, I present more details of the time line specific to this chapter:

2000 BC through AD 30	The Old Covenant of the Law
AD 30–2330	The New Covenant of Jesus on earth prior to transitioning to heaven. This entire period called the "end times" will consist of a corrupted church that people will have to maneuver through to find Jesus (Daniel 6:8, 6:12, 6:15; 8:3–13; 1 John 2:18–19; Revelation 21:1–3; Romans 10:12; Luke 21:24).
AD 30–1330*	The reign of the beast—the RCC. The RCC controls the words of Jesus and the church for 1,300 years.
AD 1330–2330	The reign of Jesus over his church. Jesus returns to earth to free his words from the control of false teachers and reign over his church. (Revelation 8:1, 20:4)
2330–eternity	The Eternal Church with God and his people (Revelation 21).

* AD 1330 is when John Wycliffe was born. He translated the Bible to English for all to read, thereby, freeing the words of Jesus from the control of the beast, RCC.

CHAPTER 8

But It's Only "About Half an Hour"

*W*E STARTED TO UNRAVEL Revelation 8:1 and we made progress by defining and determining the meaning of *silence in heaven,* but we did not complete our analysis in the last chapter. There are very important interpretations and messages left to be addressed in that short verse and this chapter will complete our analysis. The "silence in heaven" corresponded to Jesus leaving heaven to rule over his church for one thousand years during the last portion of the "hour" of the New Covenant. Based on this we claimed that, unlike commonly accepted theology, Jesus returned to earth in the year AD 1330 to reign over his church. I hope you are comfortable with the scripture verification of the return of Jesus because we will pick up the gauntlet here and finish our discussion.

We will start our continuation of the analysis by repeating this message-packed verse:

> When he opened the seventh seal, there was silence in heaven for about half an hour. (Revelation 8:1)

We conclusively determined that the "about half an hour of silence" corresponded to a period of one thousand years. There are two other very important messages to be unraveled yet. First, we will deal with the split New Covenant and explain the meaning of the word *about* from that verse. We know from the previous chapter in this book that the New Covenant is split into the following two reigns:

1. The reign of the beast that lasted from AD 30–1330, and
2. The reign of Jesus that started in AD 1330 and will last until the start of the eternal church in AD 2330.

The reign of the beast is 1,300 years long (AD 1330–30) and the reign of Jesus is stated in Revelation as being a thousand years long (AD 2330–1330). Based on all this we have the following data points:

- One hour of heaven time = 2,300 years
- The reign of the beast = 1,300 years
- The reign of Jesus = 1,000 years

Since we know that there are sixty minutes in an hour, we can perform the following simple math calculation:

- (1,000 years ÷ 2,300 years/hour of heaven) x (60 minutes/hour) = 26 minutes of Jesus' reign

I hope you don't find it strange that prophecy has just informed us all that Jesus' reign on earth with his martyrs will last twenty-six minutes when considered in heaven time, and in heaven twenty-six minutes is "about half an hour"! On the flip side, the reign of the great false church that ended in AD 1330 lasted for 1,300 years so we have another calculation:

- (1,300 years ÷ 2,300 years/hour of heaven) x (60 minutes/hour) = 33.9 minutes of beast reign

The reign of the great false church we will come to know as the beast and the RCC is 33.9 minutes and considered in heaven times this is also "about half an hour"! We now know why the Lord was specific when he told John that the silence in heaven would be for *about* half an hour rather than exactly half an hour. Prophecy together with scripture has helped us confirm the meaning of Revelation 8:1. We have verified that through a mathematical analysis of the numbers presented in scripture that the end times was prophesized to be split into two unequal portions of time that will each last "about half an hour" when considered in heaven time!

But the second message of this verse is the one that you should pay very close attention to—especially if you are reading this book as a nonbeliever in Jesus—because this message is directed at you. Many years ago, it used to be common to hear on TV, and even at the movie theater, that there would be a pause announced by, "And now, a word from our sponsor." Revelation 8:1 has a message and is flashing red lights at you to warn you that you now have a word from our sponsor—God. God, our sponsor and creator, wants you to pay special attention to this next analysis because, if you ignore the message, one day you will deeply regret it.

Remember when we said that heaven is full of praising of Jesus and is a very noisy place and we asked you whether you

would be happy in heaven if you are not into praising Jesus? We then asked you why you would even want to go to heaven if you are not praising Jesus while you are alive on earth. If you answered that without evaluating the other side of that coin, you are really messing up. There are only two options for you when you die; you will either go to heaven or you will go to hell. If you feel like you would be more comfortable in hell, please go back and read my first book, *Course Corrections to Faith and Identify the Real Gospel Authors,* that captured my short, near-twenty-four hour visit to hell. I documented my visit to hell in that first book so, as I put it, "to scare the hell out of you," because hell is a terrible place. I spend most of my time now investigating the Bible and writing summaries that prove to you that Jesus is the way to heaven because of my visit to hell. Now, to the hidden message in Revelation 8:1.

Let's look at that term *about half an hour* in greater detail and do some more math. I know many of you aren't excited about the math part but it's necessary to understand the full impact of what God has revealed. With one hour of heaven time equal to 2,300 years on earth, we have one hour in heaven equal to approximately 20 million earth hours:

- 1 hour of heaven time = 2,300 years x 365 earth days/year x 24 hours/day = 20,148,000 hours

The bottom line is that those 20,148,000 hours on earth will be like spending one hour in heaven or hell. You're wrong if you think "hell time" is any different than heaven time—the experience will be different, but the time correspondence will be the same.

Therefore, if you don't think hell will be a bad place, plan on one hour in hell being like 20 million hours on earth. God has just given you a taste of eternity. Now consider the details of my visit to hell that I already mentioned. I only *visited* hell for about a day or so, but it was such a painful experience that it seemed like eternity. Imagine being punished for 20 million hours and you are just getting started! Dwell on that for just a bit and consider being sentenced to hard labor, confined to a cell, or enclosed in a grave, or even being burned alive for 20,000,000 hours, with the knowledge that time keeps passing by and what you are experiencing will *never go away*—it's just getting started. The pain you experience in hell will last forever—it will *never* go away and never end. Should you reject Jesus, you are stuck in a place of punishment where, as Jesus says, there is weeping and gnashing of teeth and the fire never goes out (Matthew 8:12, 13:42, 13:50, 25:30).

Do you want to face a torturous existence in hell forever because you failed to research and understand the true message of Jesus? You think God isn't fair? He put a system in place where *it might seem* like bad people get away with their antics, but this is the great equalizer. Based on this and this alone, you might reconsider ignoring the story of Jesus and take the time to research and understand exactly what Jesus can do for you. You only have two choices; and, if you reject Jesus, you are considered by God to be following evil no matter what good deeds you think you may have done. Reject Jesus and there aren't enough good deeds to get you into heaven. You might say that there is no proof of God, but if so, you have missed God through creation, God through scripture, and especially now, God through predicting and fulfilling the future. If you still ignore God, there

is nothing I can say to you; however, I do pity you for choosing eternity in hell over eternal peace with God in heaven. Yes, it is a choice, and the choice is yours.

CHAPTER 9

An Introduction to Daniel

E HAVE COMPLETED OUR analysis of specific scripture verses from Revelation that help provide the foundation for understanding Daniel. Now it's time to start digging deeper into the book of Daniel to analyze prophecy verse by verse. We have already addressed some Daniel prophecy with the assistance of "borrowed" scripture from John the Apostle's book of Revelation, and as we proceed, we will continue to rely on support from the prophecy John received and documented in his book. In addition, as necessary, we will refer to the concepts we presented in the previous chapters of this book.

Our intent is to *completely* cover the book of Daniel from cover to cover. If we skip verses, it is because Daniel is repeating an earlier message, or what has been presented needs no detailed explaining. Nonetheless, we *will not skip* any verses because they might seem impossible to interpret—the Holy Spirit has walked me through Daniel in its entirety and we have spent much time in prayer and long hours of study to provide you a complete and thorough analysis. Note that I used the term *impossible* because chapters ten and eleven of Daniel contain many historical details that could be interpreted through days and weeks of research, but I decided that except for select passages in those chapters that pertain to Jesus, I will leave that analysis to others who enjoy studying history. Chapters ten and

eleven are not impossible but they will require meticulous verification through numerous resources of history books and the lack of verification of those details *do not* affect the ability to determine and understand the rest of Daniel's book.

In general, the visions and vision interpretations presented and discussed in Daniel tell us about the covenants between God and his people. In those visions and interpretations, Daniel informs us that there is an ongoing spiritual battle between good and evil and God is using his angels to help battle the evil forces in this world. In addition to visions and vision interpretations, Daniel captured two major death-defying events; Daniel's friends survived being thrown into a hot furnace and Daniel cheated a death sentence of being eaten by hungry lions. Both these events were presented by Daniel to let readers know the following three important lessons:

1. Only the one true God of heaven can save you from a death sentence that cannot be repealed or changed. Every person alive has an irrevocable and unchangeable death sentence that only God can repeal, and he does that through the saving grace of his Son, Jesus!

2. God uses "course corrections" to influence people to change their behavior. Frequently, these course corrections are painful experiences that provide a sampling of the hopelessness of the eternal damnation awaiting those who refuse to change and follow the Lord.

3. Finally, God lets rulers know through his interaction that he is in charge; rulers govern not by their own doing, they rule only because God has allowed them to.

Daniel reaffirms that only a relationship with God can give you internal and eternal peace. Daniel presents a prime example of what God expects from his interaction with each of us:

> Now I, Nebuchadnezzar, praise and exalt the King of heaven, because everything he does is right and all his ways are just. And those who walk in pride he is able to humble. (Daniel 4:37)

Nebuchadnezzar was a very powerful ruler who rejected God's course corrections, so God gave him one that completely humbled him, and this resulted in him converting from pagan worship to follow God. Through Daniel's experiences, we learned that God has been providing course corrections to draw people near to God since the beginning of time and this will continue until the time of the end. God is faithful, true, and is always with us and that means that God's promise of eternal salvation and peace is *permanently* decreed (Daniel 12:2). Finally, God prescribed the events and future of the world in advance so if you think you can change the set times and set events decreed by God, you are mistaken.

The book of Daniel is a biography of Daniel, a young man "without defect, handsome, showing aptitude for every kind of learning, well informed," who was taken prisoner by a Babylonian king who conquered Jerusalem (Daniel 1:1–4) in 605 BC. Upon his arrival in Babylonia, Daniel was placed into a three-year training period to prepare him to enter the service of the Babylonian King Nebuchadnezzar. The young men training for this king's service were fed food and wine that Daniel believed to be against God's laws given to the Jews, so Daniel

abstained from it to remain faithful to God (Daniel 1:5–8). This documentation indicates that Daniel dedicated himself to follow the ways of the God of Israel he was taught prior to being taken captive. The Lord had certainly chosen Daniel to be a special man of God.

Under the threat of execution for allowing an exception to the king's designated food and wine for Daniel, the chief official changed the mandated food and drink for a group of young Jewish men (Daniel 1:9–14). The change to follow the one true God of heaven was a positive one and the young men "looked healthier and better nourished than any of the young men who ate the royal food" (Daniel 1:15). Through this interaction, God demonstrated to the Babylonian chief official that following the law of Daniel's God was both beneficial and healthy, so the chief official changed their diet to follow God's commands (Daniel 1:16).

Next, we learn how the Lord blessed Daniel and his friends named Shadrach (Hananiah), Meshach (Mishael), and Abednego (Azariah) with "knowledge and understanding of all kinds." All four of these young men were blessed, but only Daniel was provided a special talent to "understand visions and dreams of all kinds" (Daniel 1:17). These four men completed their training in about 601 BC then entered King Nebuchadnezzar's service:

> At the end of the time set by the king to bring
> them into his service, the chief official present-
> ed them to Nebuchadnezzar. The king talked
> with them, and he found none equal to Daniel,
> Hananiah, Mishael, and Azariah; so they entered

the king's service. In every matter of wisdom and understanding about which the king questioned them, he found them ten times better than all the magicians and enchanters in his whole kingdom. (Daniel 1:18–20)

After their three years of training were completed, Daniel and his friends entered the king's service as so-called "wise men," but these four young men were special—King Nebuchadnezzar "found *them* ten times better than all the magician and enchanters in his whole kingdom." Daniel and his friends were special because God had blessed them with an abundance of insight and knowledge.

Daniel closes out his introduction with an important verse that helps assemble Daniel's time line of events and, in addition, provides a clue that helps to clear up a discrepancy found in Daniel 5:31. We will address this discrepancy next, but first we present the last verse of chapter one of Daniel:

> And Daniel remained there until the first year of
> King Cyrus (Daniel 1:21)

Daniel remained in the service of the wise men until the first year of King Cyrus and we know from history books that this is the year 539 BC. This verse is letting readers know that Daniel remained in the category of wise men servants for sixty-two years from 601 BC to 539 BC. That's a lot of history so it's an appropriate time to present the order of kings who reigned over Daniel during his lifetime.

According to various records, we have the following succession of rulers during the Babylonian reign:

605–561 BC – Nebuchadnezzar

561–560 BC – Evil Merodach

559–556 BC – Neriglissar

556 BC – Labasi Marduk

555–542 BC – Nabonidus

542–539 BC – Belshazzar

The historical accounting of the years of Babylonian kings is consistent within a year or so by most people I reviewed who have summarized it. There is one noteworthy contradiction with the book of Daniel contained in most historical ruler summaries—they claim that Belshazzar's reign lasted only one year. From Daniel 8:1, we know that Belshazzar ruled for three years and since we believe scripture, we have compensated for this by adjusting Nabonidus' and Belshazzar's reigns accordingly.

Daniel also presents events and visions while captive under the Persian Kings Darius and Cyrus. Therefore, we present the historically recorded reigns of Persian kings throughout Daniel's lifetime:

539–530 BC – Cyrus the Great

530–522 BC – Cambyses II

522 BC – Bardiya

522–486 – Darius I the Great

Daniel records a vision in the first year of Darius' reign (Daniel 9:1) and from this data we know that Daniel would be about ninety-three years old. But wait, the following scripture provides an apparent discrepancy between Daniel 1:21 and the following verses, specifically Daniel 5:31:

And that very night Belshazzar, king of the
Babylonians, was slain, and Darius the Mede
took over the kingdom, at the age of sixty-two.
(Daniel 5:30–31)

The discrepancy is obvious—this verse seems to indicate
that Darius the Mede took over in 539 BC rather than Cyrus.
Theologians try to explain this by claiming Cyrus might also
be called Darius or there might have been another ruler named
Darius prior to Cyrus physically taking over the kingdom. With
this in mind, the events Daniel describes that happened during
Darius' reign—the lion's den event and the vision of the seventy
sevens—happened much earlier than 522 BC. But this makes no
sense because, as we presented earlier, those two events provided Daniel the wisdom to understand his visions at the ripe
old age of about ninety-three. Neither of the proposed theological explanations for Darius can be verified through history
and we will tell you why—because they aren't true. King Cyrus
conquered the Babylonian kingdom and became the ruler from
539 BC to 530 BC and King Darius ruled later from 522 BC for
about forty years.

To address this discrepancy, let's first assemble the data
tracking Daniel's work life according to what we know from
scripture in his book. In the order presented in Daniel's book,
we find that Daniel—

- enters the service of the wise men (Daniel 1:18) in 601
  BC,

- remains with the wise men until the first year of Cyrus (Daniel 1:21) that we know from historical records is 539 BC,
- is promoted by Nebuchadnezzar to administrator over the wise men (Daniel 2:48) in 600 BC,
- is promoted by Belshazzar to third-highest ruler in the kingdom (Daniel 3:29) in 539 BC,
- then, according to (Daniel 6:3) so distinguished himself among the three administrators that Darius considers setting him over the whole kingdom.

From this data we know that the same day in 539 BC that Daniel is promoted by Belshazzar to the third-highest position in the kingdom is the same day Daniel was *formerly* in charge of the wise men, and it is the same day that Cyrus overthrows the kingdom and becomes Daniel's boss. This verifies that Daniel 1:18, 1:21, 2:48, and 3:29 are all true. This also means that Daniel 5:30–31 *must* be in error, unless Darius is another name for Cyrus.

We look for the possibility that Cyrus was also called Darius starting with summaries of these two rulers from the Encyclopedia Britannica online:

> Cyrus was born between 590 and 580 BCE, either in Media or, more probably, in Persia, the modern Fars province of Iran.

> Darius I, by name Darius the Great, (born 550– died 486 BC), king of Persia in 522–486 BC, one of the greatest rulers of the Achaemenid

dynasty, who was noted for his administrative genius and for his great building projects.

I searched for the Persian leader Cyrus' birth and there were several sites listing the estimated year of his birth at around 600 BC. Daniel 5:31 claims that Darius "took over the kingdom, at the age of sixty-two." Historians aren't sure exactly when Cyrus was born but simple math (600 − 539 = 61 years old) tells us with this estimated birth year Cyrus would have been right about sixty-two years old when he took reign over the former Babylonian kingdom. There isn't even a small chance that Darius was sixty-two, but there is a very good possibility that Cyrus was sixty-two when he took over the kingdom in 539 BC. Also, note that Darius is known for his "administrative genius," and we read that in Daniel 6:1–3 that Darius recognizes Daniel's expertise and abilities because he is considering appointing Daniel to administer over the entire kingdom—the number one and highest position of authority. This certainly seems to support the historical Darius who was in charge when Daniel experienced those two events.

How do we explain the error in Daniel 5:31? We don't because it's above my pay grade. However, I can speculate that Daniel, at ninety-three years old was assembling his book and needed a sentence to connect the previous account in chapter five that occurred in 539 BC to the story of the lion's den that occurred in 522 BC. Daniel added that sentence to help the transition cover those years, but he accidentally wrote Darius rather than Cyrus as he intended. Yes, scripture is inspired by God and Daniel's book is full of details proving this, but Daniel was human too and could have made this simple error.

Rewriting the data points above in the following manner results in Daniel's book making complete sense. Daniel—

- enters the service of the wise men (Daniel 1:18) in 601 BC,
- then is promoted by Nebuchadnezzar as administrator over the wise men (Daniel 2:48) in 600 BC,
- is promoted by Belshazzar to the third-highest ruler in the kingdom (Daniel 3:29) the same day that Cyrus took over the kingdom (Daniel 1:21) in 539 BC. In summary, during this day, Daniel is first in charge of the wise men, then later that day he is elevated to the third-highest position in the kingdom, then that day ends with his boss Belshazzar killed and Cyrus becomes his new boss. What a day!
- so distinguished himself during his seventeen years (539–522) as one of the three administrators over the kingdom that when Darius starts to rule in 522 BC, Darius considers setting him over the whole kingdom (Daniel 6:3).

This summary we just presented makes sense with history, makes sense for a progression of Daniel's life, and makes sense for the aspect of him finally understanding his visions at age ninety-three in the first year of Darius, and putting his life story together in his book.

In just a few moments, we are going to summarize the events presented in Daniel's book according to how they are presented, and you will see from this summary that they *are not presented chronologically—they are presented to tell a story of redemption*—the fulfillment of Jeremiah 31:31–34. Prior to this summary, we need to address two final verses of scripture because they contain an important detail that provides a good estimate of the dates of Daniel's life events:

> In the second year of his reign, Nebuchadnezzar
> had dreams; his mind was troubled and he could
> not sleep. So the king summoned the magicians,
> enchanters, sorcerers, and astrologers to tell him
> what he had dreamed. (Daniel 2:1–2)

The second year of Nebuchadnezzar's reign is 604 BC, if we take the meaning of this scripture to apply to Nebuchadnezzar alone; with Nebuchadnezzar's reign starting in 605 BC, this vision occurs while Daniel has just started training as a boy who is about eleven years old. This is not at all likely, because Daniel is not yet one of the wise men during this event. Therefore, this event cannot describe Nebuchadnezzar's reign so it *must be* referring to the reign of Nebuchadnezzar *over Daniel*. Daniel is reporting here that Nebuchadnezzar had this vision in the second year *after Daniel* went into this king's service—the second year of Nebuchadnezzar's reign over Daniel. The second year of Nebuchadnezzar's rule over Daniel in the king's service would have been in 600 BC and, at that time, Daniel is a rookie wise man of about fifteen years old.

We now conclude this chapter with the promised high-level summary of the events captured in Daniel's book. Based on,

- what we know, understand, and have presented in chapters one through three of this book about vision interpretations,

- along with the concepts presented in chapters four through eight,
- in addition to some information borrowed from later chapters, we present the following introductory summary of the book of Daniel:
- *Nebuchadnezzar's Dream of a Statue (Daniel chapter two)—600 BC:* This dream provides details about the future changes to come to the kingdom of God on earth. From the beginning, God decreed specific changes to his kingdom on earth and these prophesized changes, except for the eternal kingdom that has yet to arrive, are now proven to have been fulfilled. This vision is not about regional or ethnic kingdoms as many theologians have proposed, it is entirely about the kingdom of God on earth and the ongoing spiritual battles that will take place.

  First, there will be the kingdom of gold represented by Nebuchadnezzar who would eventually leave his pagan ways to follow the one true God of heaven. After Nebuchadnezzar's kingdom of gold, the reign over the kingdom of God on earth will be inferior. A few rulers, Darius and Cyrus, during the lifetime of Daniel will follow God (Daniel 6:28), but in general the rest will follow their pagan ways. After the inferior kingdom will come a reign of terror from a ruler pretending to be God. The kingdom of bronze will appear as though it is God, but it isn't—it is a cheap imitation. Sometime during the time of these former kingdoms, the Messiah will come to establish his kingdom with the strength of iron. The Messiah will rule over a mixed kingdom of iron and baked clay then, at the time of the end, the Messiah will remove all kingdoms and establish his eternal kingdom that will last forever.

At the time of this vision, Daniel was told what it meant; but he was still a rookie wise man threatened with death—he didn't really understand the full context of this vision and was elated with the outcome.

- *A Course Correction for Nebuchadnezzar—The Furnace (Daniel chapter three)—597 BC:* Daniel's friends are thrown into an extremely hot furnace of fire for failing to worship a pagan statue built by Nebuchadnezzar, but they are not harmed by the flames. This course correction initially seems to convert the king to worship the one true God of heaven, but it fails to change the heart of Nebuchadnezzar. The vision demonstrates God's power and influence over people and those who rule. In addition, the Holy Spirit is providing a message of redemption for the people of God who face a certain death. Daniel's friends were condemned to death for their faith in God and dedication to following the law of God, but their dedication to God spared them from a death sentence. Does this sound like the Messiah Daniel will be told about later? Daniel did not recognize this connection to the saving power of the Messiah until 522 BC when he was ninety-three years old, but he presented it early as an indication that he was being told of the saving grace of the Messiah when he was about eighteen years old.

- *An Effective Course Correction for King Nebuchadnezzar—A Dream of a Tree (Daniel chapter four)— 595 BC:* King

Nebuchadnezzar professed to be following the one true God, but he did not. God provides this king another course correction that will change this king's heart so that he will leave his pagan ways. God uses punishment to get the attention of this king and it works. This vision again has a reference to the Messiah as the tree of life that we can easily see from the book of Revelation, but Daniel again did not understand the full context of this vision until 522 BC in the first year of Darius. Like my visions, Daniel found an immediate connection of this course correction to Nebuchadnezzar's punishment, but failed to recognize the big picture.

- *Course Correction for a Rebellious King—The Writing on the Wall (Daniel chapter five) —539 BC:* Daniel had just presented two messages of redemption—his friends' lives were spared through their dedication to God and Nebuchadnezzar's reign was restored *after* he rejected other gods and dedicated himself to the one true God of heaven. Now, Daniel presents a story of the death and destruction experienced for those who reject God. Belshazzar, a descendant of Nebuchadnezzar who becomes ruler, does not follow the Lord. God works on the heart of this king to no avail. In response, God writes a death sentence for Belshazzar who, out of arrogance, mocks God by promoting Daniel for delivering the king a message of death and destruction. The writing on the wall is fulfilled when King Belshazzar is executed and his kingdom is taken by the Persians.

- *Course Correction to King Darius—The Lion's Den (Daniel chapter six)—522 BC:* In contrast to the previous story about a death sentence for those who reject the Lord, Daniel is presented another story of redemption—just in case the other two didn't stick in his mind. Daniel is an old man who has had a relatively successful life and has remained faithful to God throughout his life. However, at this ripe old age of ninety-three, Daniel has not seen the promise of the redemption for the people of Israel fulfilled. Daniel is condemned through an unbreakable decree of the Medes and Persians, but his death sentence is repealed by God. Daniel has been faithful to God and there is no doubt that it is God who spares the life of Daniel because of his dedication to God. Does this sound like the promise of the Messiah? Daniel is about to receive more visions that will help him put all the pieces together—the seventy sevens. But first, Daniel provides two visions that present a description of how the promise of redemption by God will overrule the decrees of physical death by rogue evil rulers.

- *Daniel's Vision of the Beasts—Kingdom of God Transitions (Daniel chapter seven)—541 BC:* After the Messiah comes, the kingdom will change—Daniel recognized this only after receiving his vision of the seventy sevens (Daniel 9:24–27). The time of the Messiah will not be a time of peace. The focus of this vision is on the rebuilt kingdom "in times of trouble" (Daniel 9:25). Daniel's vision focuses on the beasts who rule during the kingdom of bronze, then presents the transition to the rule of Jesus during the kingdom of iron/clay. The vision concludes with a brief prediction of the eternal kingdom at the time of

the end. The kingdom of the Messiah will be a time of trouble but his "kingdom is one that will never end."

- *Daniel's Vision of the Ram and Goat—More Kingdom of God Transitions (Daniel chapter eight)—539 BC:* Daniel receives another vision during the reign of Belshazzar and this vision details the complete transition of the kingdom of God on earth. This Old Covenant will transition to the New Covenant, then the kingdom of God will be taken over by an evil entity that will say they are God. Like the previous vision during the reign of Belshazzar, who was a corrupt and worthless ruler, there is a focus on the corrupt and worthless rulers during the kingdom of bronze. This vision provides the complete details of the transition of the Old Covenant to the New Covenant through Jesus, then wraps up the message with details of the future arrival of the everlasting kingdom—that very special verse Daniel 8:14 we addressed earlier.

- *Daniel's Vision of the Seventy Sevens—It's All about the Messiah (Chapter nine)—522 BC:* Finally—the vision that cleared it all up for Daniel. Daniel is distraught that he has not witnessed the fulfillment of a promise made to Jeremiah for the redemption for the people of Israel, so he prays to God. God removed the kingdom of Israel in 605 BC and, based on Jeremiah's prophecy of the seventy years for redemption, the Israelites thought that their kingdom would physically be restored in 535 BC. In the instant Daniel received this vision at the ripe old age of about ninety-three, the meaning of Daniel's visions and interpretations became crystal clear. The promised redemption for God's people was not through the return of an earthly kingdom for the people of Israel, it would be fulfilled by a coming Messiah who would permanently remove sin and eventually establish his eternal kingdom for the people of God. The earthly kingdom for the people of Israel will not be returned, but there is a better deal—all the people of the world will have access to redemption and salvation through the coming Messiah.

- *Daniel's Vision of the Spiritual Battle of the Kingdom of God (Chapters ten to twelve)—535 BC:* Daniel ends his book with the vision he received about thirteen years before that he now recognizes as the answer to the seventy-year promise to Jeremiah. This vision fulfilled the promise to Jeremiah by providing all the details of the future redemption and salvation of God's people through the rest of the kingdom of silver and through the kingdoms of bronze and iron/clay, and including the eternal kingdom—the rock that destroys all the other kingdoms. Wow! Daniel finally understood the full meaning of this vision that provided the full message of redemption for anyone who accepts the offer of redemption provided by God. This vision captures the complete future of the people of God and the spiritual battle they will fight throughout the future. The road for the people who dedicate themselves to God will not be an easy path, but in the end those who are victorious over evil will be considered righteous and will be redeemed.

The twelve chapters of Daniel are packed so full of details that it is nearly impossible to capture all the hidden messages, even though we have tried. Daniel specifically selected how to assemble his book based on his experiences in the first year

of Darius when he was about ninety-three years old. We do not know how long Daniel lived in the kingdom of Darius because he didn't tell us. We do know that Daniel only understood his visions *after* his redemption from a decreed certain death sentence (Daniel chapter six) and he received the vision of the Messiah who would implement redemption from death sentences for all the people of the world (Daniel chapter nine). Both these events occurred in 522 BC.

We have not been able to provide all the supporting data for our summary above, so I'll ask you to be patient as we continue our verse-by-verse review and as we continue down our journey, I will attempt to point out the connections along the way. We present the following details of Daniel's time line data obtained from this chapter:

Estimate year of Daniel's birth	c.615 BC
Nebuchadnezzar invades Judah and takes Daniel hostage	605 BC
Nebuchadnezzar's reign	605–561 BC
Daniel enters training for three years	604–601 BC
Daniel enters as a wise man into Nebuchadnezzar's service	601 BC
Daniel remains in the service of the kings as a wise man	601–539 BC
Daniel's second year of service, Nebuchadnezzar has a statue dream	600 BC
Nebuchadnezzar builds an enormous pagan gold statue	600–598 BC
Daniel's friends are thrown into a hot furnace and survive	597 BC
Nebuchadnezzar's dream of the tree of life	595 BC
Nebuchadnezzar dies	561 BC

Kings Merodach, Neriglissar, Marduk, and Nabonidus rule	561–542 BC
King Belshazzar rules	542–539 BC
Daniel's vision of the New Covenant with focus on the beast	541 BC
Daniel's vision of the New Covenant with focus on the ram and goat	539 BC
King Cyrus the Persian overthrows Belshazzar and the Babylonians	539 BC
Daniel's vision in fulfillment of Jeremiah's seventy-year promise	535 BC
Daniel and his lesson in the lion's den	522 BC
Daniel's vision of the coming Messiah	522 BC

CHAPTER 10

The Kingdom

WE CONTINUE WITH THE story of Daniel who is now a rookie in the group of wise men (Daniel 1:18). The ruler, Nebuchadnezzar, has a dream that troubles the king (Daniel 2:1) so he brought all the wise men together to ask them for the meaning of this vision (Daniel 2:2–3). In response to Nebuchadnezzar's request, the astrologers took the lead and stalled for time while buttering up the king, then the astrologers requested that the king tell the wise men what the dream was about (Daniel 2:4). This king was no fool—he didn't want the wise men to make up a story based on what Nebuchadnezzar revealed, so he required the group of wise men to tell him what the dream was *and* what it meant:

> The king replied to the astrologers, "This is what I have firmly decided: If you do not tell me what my dream was and interpret it, I will have you cut into pieces and your houses turned into piles of rubble." (Daniel 2:5)

We learn from this passage that King Nebuchadnezzar is a brutal ruler who uses intimidation and death threats to govern the people; he is impulsive and hotheaded, and this is not a good combination —especially for those in his service.

The astrologers tried to stall for more time to resolve their lethal problem, but it didn't work—the king remained firm in his demand for them to describe his dream and provide the interpretation of it (Daniel 2:6–9). Then, the astrologers opened their mouths again:

> What the king asks is too difficult. No one can reveal it to the king except the gods, and they do not live among humans. This made the king so angry and furious that he ordered the execution of all the wise men of Babylon. (Daniel 2:11–12)

This time, the tactic of the astrologers made the king so mad that he ordered the execution of all the wise men in his service. As a side note, you will later see how the astrologers are an evil bunch of pagans (Daniel 3:8).

Daniel, his three friends, and the rest of the wise men are going to be put to death unless they can reveal and interpret the king's dream. As the commander of the king's guard was getting ready to execute the wise men (Daniel 2:14), Daniel requested time with the king and asked for additional time to solve the mystery the king presented (Daniel 2:15–16). This was a brave move made by Daniel who risked death by even requesting a delay. Daniel was granted his request and returned to his house to join with his friends in prayer:

> Then Daniel returned to his house and explained the matter to his friends Hananiah, Mishael, and Azariah. He urged them to plead for mercy from the God of heaven concerning this mystery, so that he and his friends might not be executed

with the rest of the wise men of Babylon. (Daniel 2:17–18)

Daniel and his friends communicated with God every day in prayer; we get confirmation of this later in Daniel's accounts of these four men receiving death sentences because they hold true to God in prayer. Telling the king the contents and meaning of Nebuchadnezzar's dream is impossible unless you are talking to the one true God every day and he is on your side. If you read the language in this verse carefully you notice that Daniel and his friends did not like being associated with the wise men. Daniel infers that they don't mind if the rest of the wise men of Babylon are executed—they just don't want to be included (so that he and his friends might not be executed with the rest of the wise men of Babylon). This is likely because Daniel and his friends are Jews following the one true God of heaven, and the rest of the wise men are pagans who worship and follow many gods.

Also, please note that Daniel's reference to God is to the "God of heaven," rather than to the "God of Israel" because Israel no longer exists—the wrath of God has been poured out on Israel for their disobedience and the kingdom of Israel was removed from the earth in 605 BC. The people of Israel still exist under the reign of foreign rulers, but the kingdom of Israel has been extinguished. This is an important detail as we proceed because Daniel and the rest of the Jews expected the kingdom to be returned to Israel in seventy years corresponding to 535 BC, as promised by God to the prophet Jeremiah (Jeremiah 31:31–34).

God answers the prayers of Daniel:

During the night the mystery was revealed to Daniel in a vision. Then Daniel praised the God of heaven and said: "Praise be to the name of God for ever and ever; wisdom and power are his." (Daniel 2:19–20)

After Daniel's talk with the Lord, his prayers were answered in a vision, so Daniel worships and thanks the Lord for his interaction (Daniel 2:21–22). Daniel then gets specific in his thankfulness to the Lord:

I thank and praise you, God of my ancestors. You have given me wisdom and power. You have made known to me what we asked of you, you have made known to us the dream of the king." (Daniel 2:23)

Daniel certainly learned how God interacted with the people of Israel in the past (God of my ancestors) and now Daniel thanks God for continuing to interact with the people of God through him (You have given me wisdom and power). Daniel gives all the credit to God for responding to the prayers of the four men (You have made known to me what *we* asked of you) and now Daniel understands both, what the king's dream was and what it means.

Just before the king's order to execute the wise men is carried out, Daniel finds the executioner and requests a meeting with the king (Daniel 2:24–25). Daniel is granted a visit with the king and when the king asks about the dream (Daniel 2:26), Daniel responds with the following:

> Daniel replied, "No wise man, enchanter, magician, or diviner can explain to the king the mystery he has asked about, but there is a God in heaven who reveals mysteries. He has shown King Nebuchadnezzar what will happen in the days to come. (Daniel 2:27–28)

Daniel informs the king that no pagan can "explain to the king the mystery he has asked about"— there is only one true God who has power over all and that is the "God in heaven who reveals mysteries." Daniel informs King Nebuchadnezzar that the dream God gave to Nebuchadnezzar is about the future (what will happen in the days to come).

In summary thus far, Daniel's gift from the Holy Spirit to interpret dreams became known when King Nebuchadnezzar had a dream and threatened the wise men in his service with a horrible execution if they could not tell the king both what the dream was and what it meant. Daniel was one of these wise men. Daniel prayed to God, then just prior to his scheduled execution, God provided Daniel the details and meaning of Nebuchadnezzar's vision. Based on Daniel's answer to prayer he approached the executioner and asked for a meeting with the king to tell Nebuchadnezzar the details and meaning of his dream. Daniel met with the king and explained to him that no pagan god could grant him the details and meaning of his vision, but the one true God of heaven can and in fact did.

Daniel is now going to tell Nebuchadnezzar the details of his dream:

As your majesty was lying there, your mind turned to things to come, and the revealer of mysteries showed you what is going to happen. As for me, this mystery has been revealed to me, not because I have greater wisdom than anyone else alive, but so that Your Majesty may know the interpretation and that you may understand what went through your mind. (Daniel 2:29–30)

God lets Daniel know that the king's dream is about the future—he does not say how far in the future —just that God is showing the king "things to come." Notice that Daniel informs the king in a very smooth manner that God is working in this king and wants him to know "what is going to happen." We learn that Daniel is:

- humbled by the presence of God in his life and lets this king know it (As for me, this mystery has been revealed to me, not because I have greater wisdom than anyone else alive);
- giving God credit but is very careful with his words so as not to upset the hotheaded king (but so that *Your majesty* may know the interpretation); and,
- following the Holy Spirit to use this opportunity to share the comfort the God of heaven provides to those who follow him (and that you may understand what went through your mind).

Then, Daniel provides the king the details of his dream:

> Your majesty looked, and there before you stood
> a large statue—an enormous, dazzling statue,
> awesome in appearance. The head of the stat-
> ue was made of pure gold, its chest and arms
> of silver, its belly and thighs of bronze, its legs
> of iron, and its feet partly of iron and partly of
> baked clay. (Daniel 2:31–33)

There are current interesting theories and interpretations on the meaning of the portions of the statue and all seem to center around and focus on kingdoms of the world, with the Babylonian as the gold, Medo-Persia as the silver, Greece as the bronze, and the Roman kingdom as the iron and clay mixture. The attempts of theologians to box this vision into nice categories of ethnic kingdoms fail because God does not care about ethnicity and rule—God is only concerned about his kingdom on earth and who he has appointed to rule over it.

Through my visions and answers to prayers I found that the statue is not about earthly kingdoms, it is *all* about God's kingdom on earth. Yes, there will be distinct periods of ethnic rulers over the land, but this vision God provided Daniel will not be about named earthly regional kingdoms who rule, it will be a description of who God has appointed to rule his kingdom throughout the two covenants he made with his people. Very early in my investigation into prophecy, the Holy Spirit told me that prophecy in the books of Daniel and Revelation are all about the church—the kingdom of God on earth. We get confirmation of this fact in the vision of the statue. As a side note, I will include and address those visions that guided me to this

complete review of prophecy in the follow-up book that completes the interpretation of the book of Revelation.

At first glance, the statue appears to have five distinct kingdoms described; one of gold, silver, bronze, iron, and iron mixed with clay. Then, I received a vision from the Holy Spirit to help me out:

> March 12, 2023—I have an electric wire problem I'm trying to work out. How many power wires and ground wires will be in the cable? Will there be four power wires and two ground wires or five power wires and two ground wires, or even something else? I went up to ask a woman in front of the group.

Hmm . . . my initial indication is that there are five kingdoms that match the materials of the statue, but here I am told there could be four—I just need to check with the "woman in front of the group." And who is the woman in front of the group? From our earlier analysis, we know that the woman is the church who is changing over time. Therefore, when I put these all together, I am looking at the transition of power in the kingdom of God on earth—his temple/church over time. In a power wire system, the power wires drive the change and the grounding wires are necessary for the power system to work. The two grounding wires in my vision tell me that there will be two necessary fundamental pieces of the kingdom of God on earth that without the temple/church will not exist.

My initial conclusion was that the head of the statue is made of pure gold signifying that there is kingdom that will follow

God, then afterwards another kingdom will arise that will be like silver—not as valuable as gold—some rulers will follow God and some will not. A third kingdom will arise that appears to be gold but is not—it is a pretender kingdom. After the pretender kingdom will come a powerful kingdom of iron, but then it will be replaced by a kingdom that is a mixture of this power together with rulers that have no connection to God—they have no strength or foundation like iron —they are an iron/clay mixture. I realized that I needed more information, so I decided to continue to the next verses and put off the interpretations of my vision of the wires and Nebuchadnezzar's vision of the statue.

Daniel then provides Nebuchadnezzar more aspects of this statue vision:

> While you were watching, a rock was cut out, but not by human hands. It struck the statue on its feet of iron and clay and smashed them. Then the iron, the clay, the bronze, the silver, and the gold were all broken into pieces and became like chaff on a threshing floor in the summer. The wind swept them away without leaving a trace. But the rock that struck the statue became a mountain and filled the whole earth. (Daniel 2:34–35)

While these kingdoms are being observed (While you were watching), God sends his Son Jesus (a rock cut out, but not by human hands). Why am I connecting the rock to Jesus? Because Jesus referred to himself as the rock in a parable (Matthew

7:24) and even Old Testament scripture in the time of Daniel verifies it:

> For I will proclaim Yahweh's name, Ascribe greatness to our God! The Rock: his work is perfect, for all his ways are just (Deuteronomy 32:3-4)

> Yahweh is my rock, my fortress, and my deliverer; my God, my rock, in who I take refuge, my shield, and the horn of my salvation, my high tower (Psalm 18:2)

It wasn't clear to Daniel just as it isn't clear to theologians now that this rock is a reference to the coming Messiah and his kingdom; Daniel never mentions this and neither do the expert theologians. This connection will become more obvious as we continue to unravel the vision of the statue.

After the mixed kingdom of the iron and clay mixture, there will be an end to the kingdoms of God on earth during the last kingdom (It struck the statue on its feet of iron and clay and smashed them). There will be no more need for kingdoms on the earth (the iron, the clay, the bronze, the silver, and the gold were all broken into pieces and became like chaff) once the rock smashes the last kingdom. If this sounds like the Messiah ushering in his eternal church (the rock that stuck the statue became a mountain) it does to me too. The eternal church will completely replace the kingdom of God on the earth (and filled the whole earth).

Immediately, after telling the king the details of the king's vision, Daniel informs the king that he will provide the king the official interpretation that we know is coming from the Holy Spirit of God:

> This was the dream, and now we will interpret it
> for the king. (Daniel 2:36)

How do we know that this interpretation is coming from the Holy Spirit of God? We read earlier in Daniel 2:25 that "Arioch took Daniel to the king," therefore, Daniel is alone with Arioch, and the king and neither one of these two people are helping Daniel with the interpretation. Daniel is letting the king know that he has help interpreting this dream—someone else will be with Daniel as he interprets this dream for the king (*we* will interpret it for the king). There is only one option to consider—Daniel is clearly referring to the presence of the Holy Spirit with him as he presents this information to the king. Just as I have been referring to *we*, indicating that the Holy Spirit is guiding me through my investigations, conclusions, and reporting of results, the Holy Spirit is guiding Daniel through his interaction with the king.

The next two verses are very important because they provide important clues that help us understand each kingdom and the power structure of my wire vision:

> Your Majesty, you are the king of kings. The God
> of heaven has given you dominion and power
> and might and glory; in your hand he has placed
> all mankind and the beasts of the field and the
> birds in the sky. Wherever they live, he has
> made you ruler over them all. You are that head
> of gold. (Daniel 2:37–38)

I had my initial assumption that the kingdom of gold was the rulers who followed God during Daniel's life but that turned out to be inaccurate. The Holy Spirit revealed to Daniel that Nebuchadnezzar is the current ruler of the kingdom of God, and *only* he is representing God during his rule. God has given all his authority and power to Nebuchadnezzar during his reign and called him, and only him, the kingdom of gold represented by the head of the statue (The God of heaven has given *you* dominion and power and might and glory). Nebuchadnezzar and *no other kings* had been considered to rule during the kingdom of gold (*You* are that head of gold). The kingdom of gold will end when Nebuchadnezzar's rule ends.

You may note from these passages that there are no *accidental rulers*. All kingdoms on earth have been permitted to rule by God (he has *made* you ruler). God is going to work wonders in Nebuchadnezzar to turn him from paganism to worship the God of heaven, then he will rule as a godly king. After I read this very clear scripture that pointed me directly to Nebuchadnezzar as the head of gold, I couldn't help but wonder how theologians concluded that the head of gold is the entire kingdom of Babylonia.

The kingdom of God on earth will change after Nebuchadnezzar's reign:

> After you, another kingdom will arise, inferior
> to yours. (Daniel 2:39)

When Nebuchadnezzar dies the kingdom of gold will be replaced by the kingdom of silver. The rulers who come after Nebuchadnezzar will not always be pagan, but they also will not be the gold standard that Nebuchadnezzar became. We are going to borrow the following verse from later in Daniel to help us define the kingdom of silver:

> So Daniel prospered during the reign of Darius and the reign of Cyrus the Persians. (Daniel 6:28)

Daniel is a man of God, therefore, there is only one possible reason for Daniel to prosper during the reign of these two rulers—they are following the one true God of heaven. From our earlier analysis, we know that many other rulers reigned over Daniel during his lifetime, but here Daniel defines the rulers that follow God as *only* Darius and Cyrus. Of the nine historical rulers during the life of Daniel, only two of them followed the Lord. This is certainly an inferior kingdom that replaced the kingdom of gold.

After the inferior kingdom of rulers, we learn of a very prominent and widespread kingdom that will rule:

> Next, a third kingdom, one of bronze, will rule over the whole earth. (Daniel 2:39)

Bronze is a material that looks like gold, but it is not. The kingdom of God will transform from a mixed kingdom of pagan worshippers sprinkled with a few who are dedicated to God, to a kingdom of pretenders. This must be a reference to the RCC that we have already stated replaced the words of Jesus with their own so they could take over the church—the pretender kingdom of bronze with a reign from AD 30 to AD 1330. This

future ruler over the kingdom of God on earth will not be with or from God, but it will act as though he is.

Next, there will be a transition to the most powerful ruler:

> Finally, there will be a fourth kingdom, strong as iron—for iron breaks and smashes everything to pieces, so it will crush and break all the others. Just as you saw that the feet and toes were partly baked clay and partly of iron, so this will be a divided kingdom; yet it will have some of the strength of iron in it, even as you saw iron mixed with clay. As the toes were partly iron and partly clay, so this kingdom will be partly strong and partly brittle. And just as you saw the iron mixed with baked clay, so the people will be a mixture and will not remain united, any more than iron mixes with clay. (Daniel 2:40–43)

The key word here is *finally*. Jesus will come to the earth to establish the fourth and final kingdom (Finally, there will be a fourth kingdom). The kingdom of Jesus will, unlike the others, be powerful (strong as iron—for iron breaks and smashes everything to pieces). The kingdom of Jesus replaces all the other kingdoms (so it will crush and break all the others), however, as written in Daniel 9:25, it will exist "in times of trouble" (so this will be a divided kingdom). We know from our previous analysis that Jesus will come with his seven-year mission to provide the foundation for the church and, in the middle, he will replace the sacrifice. Then, for the last half of the seven, Jesus will start the church through his disciples. The church of

Jesus Christ will not be unified, it will be fractured with many beliefs not coming from God (so the people will be a mixture and will not remain united).

Next, we obtain another key to help unlock the meaning of my power and ground wire vision:

> In the time of those kings, the God of heaven will set up a kingdom that will never be destroyed, nor will it be left to another people. It will crush all those kingdoms and bring them to an end, but it will itself endure forever. This is the meaning of the vision of the rock cut out of a mountain, but not by human hands—a rock that broke the iron, the bronze, the clay, the silver, and the gold to pieces. The great God has shown the king what will take place in the future. The dream is true and its interpretation is trustworthy. (Daniel 2:44–45)

During the other kingdoms (In the time of those kings), God will send Jesus to set up (the God of heaven will set up a kingdom) a permanent kingdom (that will never be destroyed) that will not be replaced or left for others—it will be the final kingdom (nor will it be left to another people). The key to that last message is that God will send the world Jesus *during* the times of those other kingdoms. Based on this, we can start to assemble our interpretations of the statue that will also address my power wire vision as it relates to the kingdoms of the statue.

1. Kingdom of gold—Nebuchadnezzar: 592–561 BC

I presented the start of the kingdom of gold as the estimated year that Nebuchadnezzar fully dedicated himself to the one true God of heaven and left behind his pagan worship practices for good. We won't get to this analysis until we examine the vision of the tree—Nebuchadnezzar's second vision that Daniel will help interpret. The kingdom of gold is only Nebuchadnezzar; therefore, it ends with his death in 561 BC. We borrowed the date of the start of the kingdom of gold from future analysis.

> 2. Kingdom of silver—Rulers that come after Nebuchadnezzar who did not always follow God: 561 BC–AD 30

We have already determined that only two of the nine rulers after Nebuchadnezzar dedicated themselves to follow God. We can assume from Daniel 6:28 and the fact that seven of nine rulers during Daniel's life were pagan worshippers that the rulers after the death of Daniel, and up to the sacrifice of Jesus, were prophesized to be mostly pagan worshippers. Rulers who follow God will be few and far between during the kingdom of silver.

> 3. Kingdom of bronze—The reign of the beast also called the RCC: AD 30–1330

After the mostly pagan period of the kingdom of silver, Jesus will come to replace the sacrifice requirements. As his church is started, false teachers will infiltrate his church and take complete control over it by replacing the words of Jesus with their own. They fully control the Word of God and the church to become the kingdom of bronze.

4. The kingdom of iron—It will be the kingdom of God through Jesus that will never be replaced—it will transform into the eternal kingdom. There will be some aspects to this kingdom explained in the statue:

Repeating from earlier:

> In the time of those kings, the God of heaven will set up a kingdom that will never be destroyed, nor will it be left to another people. (Daniel 2:44)

The fourth and final kingdom will be the coming of Jesus, and there are three aspects to this kingdom that need to be considered:

a. It will come during the time of the other kingdoms: God will send Jesus on a seven-year mission that will transition the Old Covenant to the New Covenant. Jesus will arrive in 5/6 BC in the later years of the kingdom of silver. Prior to the start of the kingdom of bronze, he will start his seven-year mission from AD 26–33. The sacrifice will be in the middle, and this will mark the end of the kingdom of silver and the beginning of the kingdom of bronze. Jesus' seven-year mission will be completed during the early years of the kingdom of bronze from AD 30–33 with the end of the protection period and the start of the church.

Jesus' kingdom of iron came during the end of the kingdom of silver and the beginning of the kingdom of bronze.

b. The kingdom of Jesus will be a split kingdom with a portion of it as the kingdom of bronze and another portion of it as the mixed iron and baked clay. This aspect of the kingdom of Jesus indicates that there will be a period of reign of Jesus among other portions of the church that remain dedicated to false teaching. We are currently in this mixed iron/baked clay kingdom of God on earth. Everywhere in the church tradition has crept into the words of Jesus. Tradition is in the church through the Gospel authors and has been injected into interpretations of prophetic scripture. Rather than the entire church and scripture pointing to Jesus, we have many references to worldly kingdoms and people. The portion of the kingdom of iron that will be mixed iron/baked clay started in AD 1330 and will continue to AD 2330 when Jesus brings his eternal church to the world.

c. The kingdom of iron never ends—it simply transforms from each of these three phases. The final phase is the arrival of the eternal church—the kingdom of God will return to the 100% pure Jesus church that existed as Jesus sacrificed himself for the sin of people.

We summarize the interpretation in the following table.

Table 1
Kingdoms of the Statue

Kingdom	Wires	Rulers	Time Frame
Gold	Power	Nebuchadnezzar	592–561 BC
Silver	Power	Babylonian, Persian, Greek, and Roman Rule	561 BC–AD 30
Bronze	Power	The RCC rules over the church	AD 30–1330
Iron	Power	The kingdom of Jesus that arrives in 5/6 BC with the seven of Jesus overlapping the silver and bronze kingdoms. It will be a split kingdom of bronze from AD 30–1330 and iron/clay Jesus reigning from AD 1330–2330.	5/6 BC– Eternity
	Grounding	Jesus' seven-year mission	5/6 BC–AD 33
	Grounding	Jesus sets up his eternal church	2330–eternity

You can see how my vision of four or five power wires together with two ground wires makes sense. You could consider the iron kingdom when Jesus came to rule to be considered two separate kingdoms because it is a split kingdom, or you could see them as two separate kingdoms. Furthermore, without the grounding wires—the seven-year mission of Jesus and the arrival of the eternal church—there is no hope. Without Jesus grounding the system, the kingdoms' church is worthless.

How's that for a beautiful beginning to the story of Daniel's visions?! As we proceed, you will see how *all* Daniel's visions tie back to this vision of the statue—God decreed specific kingdoms for his temple/church of the future. There are scripture

verses in prophecy stating that some have tried to change the set times, but they were not able to. Note that these predictions were made many years in advance and history has proven them to have come true— except for the eternal kingdom that we know will be arriving soon.

There are a few more verses to consider before we end this interpretation of the vision of the statue. Nebuchadnezzar praises Daniel and tells Daniel how great God is:

> Then King Nebuchadnezzar fell prostrate before Daniel and paid him honor and ordered that an offering and incense be presented to him. The king said to Daniel, "Surely your God is the God of gods and the Lord of kings and a revealer of mysteries for you were able to reveal this mystery." (Daniel 2:46–47)

King Nebuchadnezzar has had his first experience with the God of Daniel, but as you will soon see, he remained a pagan and did not convert. God would need to provide this king more course corrections that would convince him to become a follower and believer in the one true God of heaven.

This next verse is important because it provides that important piece of the puzzle that we used earlier to help resolve the discrepancy of the future Persian king rulers—Daniel is rewarded with a promotion:

> Then the king placed Daniel in a high position and lavished many gifts on him. He made him ruler over the entire province of Babylon and

placed him in charge of all its wise men. (Daniel 2:48)

This verse combined with Daniel 1:21 tells us that Daniel managed the wise men throughout the kingdom from approximately 600 BC when he interpreted the vision for Nebuchadnezzar until 539 BC. Daniel remained in this position of managing the wise men throughout the Babylonian kingdom for about sixty-one years until that last exciting, busy, and tumultuous day of Belshazzar's reign.

In closing out this chapter, we have several additions to the time line that we can add:

Kingdom of gold	592–561 BC
Kingdom of silver	561 BC–AD 30
Kingdom of bronze	AD 30–1330
Kingdom of iron	5/6 BC–eternity
Mixed period of iron/clay	AD 1330–2330
Eternal kingdom	AD 2330–eternity

CHAPTER 11

A "Failed" Course Correction

A S WE CONTINUE OUR analysis of the book of Daniel, we find trouble is brewing in the kingdom of Nebuchadnezzar—he has not yet converted to follow the God of heaven. Nebuchadnezzar was certainly moved by the ability of Daniel to tell this king about his statue dream and its meaning, but Nebuchadnezzar was for a long time a pagan worshipper, and old habits and practices are hard to change. We find that it is not easy for God to change the heart of Nebuchadnezzar to leave his pagan ways and follow the one true God of heaven. We left last chapter as King Nebuchadnezzar "fell prostrate before Daniel and paid him honor," and then he rewarded Daniel with a promotion to manage the wise men of the kingdom.

But wait, if you examine that last passage closely, you find that King Nebuchadnezzar is not praising God for providing the interpretation of his dream to Daniel, he *fell prostrate before Daniel and paid honor"* to him. Daniel had said exactly what King Nebuchadnezzar wanted to hear—"*you* are the king of all kings" and "in *your* hands he has placed all mankind and the beasts of the field and the birds"—and these words caused this king to believe that he was God, rather than a ruler representing God. We did see in Daniel 2:47 Nebuchadnezzar tell Daniel that "your God is the God of gods," but this indicates that Nebuchadnezzar does not consider Daniel's God to be *his*

god—Nebuchadnezzar has many gods and is not leaving his pagan ways behind. Note that Daniel did not object to the praises and worship of the king—in fact, it seems that he might have even enjoyed it—and who wouldn't mind going from facing death and walking on eggshells to becoming a trusted servant of the ruler?

Not only did Daniel enjoy the rewards he was receiving for interpreting the king's dream, he also wanted his friends to share in the benefits:

> Moreover, at Daniel's request the king appointed Shadrach, Meshach, and Abednego administrators over the province of Babylon, while Daniel himself remained at the royal court. (Daniel 2:49)

Daniel recommended to the king that his friends share in the benefits and Nebuchadnezzar honored Daniel's request and promoted Daniel's friends (at Daniel's request the king appointed Shadrach, Meshach, and Abednego administrators). Daniel remained at the royal court of the king, but his friends who were promoted were apparently relocated.

Although Daniel and his friends were promoted, they were not able to convince the hotheaded king to understand that God is in charge and only God was responsible for the king's dream and its interpretation. The vision and interpretation had not converted this king to follow God and, in fact, it had the opposite effect; in response to the vision, Nebuchadnezzar erected a pagan statue:

> King Nebuchadnezzar made an image of gold,
> sixty cubits high and six cubits wide, and set
> it up on the plain of Dura in the province of
> Babylon. (Daniel 3:1)

In response to his dreams and its interpretation,
Nebuchadnezzar built an enormous pagan worship statue. We
are not sure if the statue represented Nebuchadnezzar or if it
represented what he saw in his dream, but in either case it was
erected for pagan worship purposes. A statue of this size with a
gold finish likely took at least a few years to build, so with our
estimate of Daniel's interpretation of the vision of the statue
having occurred in 600 BC, this enormous statue was likely
completed in 598 BC.

Note that Daniel and his friends are still young men around
seventeen or eighteen years old when all this takes place, so
these four men are likely getting more and more anxiety-stricken as they see the statue being erected. Surely there is talk about
how everyone will be required to worship the statue once it is
completed. The time finally arrives and the friends of Daniel
have an "Uh-oh!" moment when the king requires everyone in
his kingdom to worship the statue (Daniel 3:2–5). It gets worse
as Nebuchadnezzar decrees that whoever fails to "fall down" at
the sound of certain musical instruments to worship the statue
will be thrown into a blazing hot fired furnace (Daniel 3:6). We
learn that this is a widespread requirement for "all the nations
and peoples of every language" (Daniel 3:7), but some of the
Jews were ignoring the command (Daniel 3:8). A group of wise
men known as the astrologers reported to the king that their
Jewish bosses, Shadrach, Meshach, and Abednego, were not

fulfilling the command to worship the statue. Remember the category of wise men who always seemed to have a voice with the king, and I called them "evil"? These are the devout pagan worshippers who loved kissing up to the king and seemed to have implied power over the rest of the wise men.

The astrologers once again praised the king then afterwards reported the Jewish leaders, Daniel's friends, for worshipping their God instead of paying homage to the pagan statue (Daniel 3:9–12). The failure of Daniel's friends to worship the statue enrages the king:

> Furious with rage, Nebuchadnezzar summoned Shadrach, Meshach, and Abednego. (Daniel 3:13)

Nebuchadnezzar was in a killing mood once he heard that the Jews who had been rewarded with a promotion, and likely had a very comfortable living, were being disobedient. Daniel, who had remained at the royal court (Daniel 2:49), was apparently not at all affected by this command. The king threatened Daniel's friends with a horrible death if they continued to disobey the king. Nebuchadnezzar even mocks the power of the God of heaven (Daniel 3:14–15).

The friends of Daniel stand their ground and turn to the God of heaven for protection:

> Shadrach, Meshach, and Abednego replied to him, "King Nebuchadnezzar, we do not need to defend ourselves before you in the matter. If we are thrown into the blazing furnace, the God we serve is able to deliver us from it, and he will

> deliver us from Your Majesty's hand. But even if
> he does not, we want you to know, Your Majesty,
> that we will not serve your gods or worship the
> image of gold you have set up." (Daniel 3:16–18)

The three men turned to the one true God for protection, but they were uncertain whether God would spare them (But even if he does not). In response, Nebuchadnezzar had the three men thrown into the furnace that was heated "seven times hotter than usual," but these men did not perish (Daniel 3:19–27). Note that "*seven* times hotter" indicates the furnace was as hot as it could get—it was a "seven"—completely heated!

The king witnessed what had happened—the God of Daniel and his friends had miraculously spared the lives of these three men. In response, Nebuchadnezzar demanded that everyone in the kingdom praise the God of heaven worshipped by Daniel and his three friends (Daniel 3:28–30). As Daniel ended this story, he did not confirm that Nebuchadnezzar converted. Nebuchadnezzar had ordered his kingdom to follow the God of Daniel and his friends, but this king was still going to rebel and wasn't quite ready to commit to the God of heaven. It will take another course correction from God to convert this ruler.

We have the following additions to the time line from this chapter:

Nebuchadnezzar erects a statue of gold for pagan worship	600–598 BC
Daniel's Jewish friends are thrown into the furnace for disobeying	597 BC

CHAPTER 12

Nebuchadnezzar's Dream of a Tree

*A*S WE BEGIN CHAPTER four of the Book of Daniel, King Nebuchadnezzar is announcing to everyone in the world (Daniel 4:1) that he is praising God. He sends out the following decree:

> It is my pleasure to tell you about the miraculous signs and wonders that the Most High God has performed for me. How great are his signs, how mighty his wonders. His kingdom is an eternal kingdom; his dominion endures from generation to generation. (Daniel 4:2–3)

But the king's praises to God are insincere. How do we know? Because the king is still a pagan worshipper. We are told that the king is lying in bed when he has a dream pass through his mind that troubles him (Daniel 4:4–5) and, in response, Nebuchadnezzar summons the *pagans* for help:

> So I commanded that all the wise men of Babylon be brought before me to interpret the dream for me. (Daniel 4:6)

Daniel with the assistance of the one true God of heaven had interpreted Nebuchadnezzar's first dream, but this king has long forgotten this fact and his knee-jerk reaction is to turn to the pagans for help. We can tell from these passages that the king has softened up a bit and is not the same king he was some years ago, because there is no threat of executions.

When these so called "wise men" fail (Daniel 4:7), Nebuchadnezzar finally summons their boss—Daniel. Nebuchadnezzar further wrote in his decree to all the nations:

> Finally, Daniel came into my presence and I told him the dream. (He is called Belteshazzar, after the name of my god, and the spirit of the holy gods is in him.)

Although Nebuchadnezzar had previously announced to the world that the "Most High God" has done wonders for this king, Daniel's God is still not the god of Nebuchadnezzar (after the name of *my* god). Furthermore, Nebuchadnezzar states that Daniel has many of the gods of the Babylonians in him (and the spirit of the holy gods is in him). Nebuchadnezzar is playing both sides of the field—pretending to believe in the one and only true God of heaven but worshipping and believing in pagan gods.

Nebuchadnezzar reaffirms his pagan beliefs (Daniel 4:9) then starts to describe his dream to Daniel:

> These are the visions I saw while lying in bed; I looked, and there before me stood a tree in the middle of the land. Its height was enormous. The tree grew large and strong and its top touched

the sky; it was visible to the ends of the earth.
(Daniel 4:10–11)

Right from the start we recognize this vision to be like the
tree of life presented in the book of Revelation. From Revelation
we have:

> Blessed are those who wash their robes, that
> they may have the right to the tree of life and
> may go through the gates into the city. Outside
> are the dogs, those who practice magic arts, the
> sexually immoral, the murderers, the idolaters,
> and everyone who loves and practices false-
> hood. (Revelation 22:14–15)

The tree of life represents the eternal kingdom of God provided to those who follow God. There is only one person who
gives access to the tree of life—Jesus (To the one who is victorious, I will give the right to eat from the tree of life). What are
we warned about to be victorious over? The evil ways of the
world (Outside are the dogs, those who practice magic arts, the
sexually immoral, the murderers, the idolaters) that will also
cause the church to become corrupted (everyone who loves
and practices falsehood). Jesus is warning us all to stay true to
his words and not to be fooled by others who will come pro-
claiming to be God. Only Jesus who is the God of heaven has
the words that will allow you to eat from the tree of life in para-
dise. To those who stick to the church founded by the disciples
(twelve crops of fruit), Jesus will give the "right to eat from the
tree of life."

But is Nebuchadnezzar's vision of the tree the same as the tree described in the book of Revelation? Yes, it is as evidenced from the following:

> Its leaves were beautiful, its fruit abundant, and
> on it was food for all. Under it the wild animals
> found shelter, and the birds lived in its branches;
> from it every creature was fed. (Daniel 4:12)

This description mirrors what John saw in his vision about the tree of life (Revelation 22:2). First, King Nebuchadnezzar tells of a vision of a tree of life with it being in the "middle of the land" with a top that "touched the sky" and is "visible to the ends of the earth" and these are clearly descriptions of the eminence of God. Then the king was shown that everyone has access to the tree of life—it is beautiful "and on it was food for all." God told Nebuchadnezzar in his previous vision that Nebuchadnezzar was a king that would follow God, and now God is telling this king that he is to bring people to God too—he is to spread the good news. Nebuchadnezzar has been told that he is representing the kingdom of gold, and this means that he is supposed to be representing Jesus to his kingdom. However, he is not fulfilling this tall order.

We know that nothing gets past God—he sees everything, and because of this, God is showing Nebuchadnezzar that he is about to be punished if he doesn't change his ways:

> In the vision I saw while lying in bed, I looked,
> and there before me was a holy one, a messen-
> ger, coming down from heaven. He called in a
> loud voice; "cut down the tree and trim off its

branches; strip off its leaves and scatter its fruit.
Let the animals flee from under it and the birds
flee from its branches. But let the stump and its
roots, bound with iron and bronze, remain in
the ground, in the grass of the field. Let him be
drenched with the dew of heaven, and let him
live with the animals among the plants of the
earth." (Daniel 4:13–15)

This king, who is failing as the representative of Jesus to the
people of God, will be humbled (cut down the tree and trim off
its branches, strip off its leaves and scatter its fruit). The king
will be deposed from leadership (Let the animals free from under it and the birds flee from its branches), but he will not be
killed (remain in the ground) and will remain among his people
(remain in the ground, and in the grass of the field).

We get another confirmation of a tie-in to Jesus through the
connection to the transition of the kingdom after Jesus per-
forms his sacrifice. Jesus will be crucified (cut down the tree
and trim off its branches) and then those starting the church
will scatter (strip off its leaves and scatter its fruit). Afterwards,
although the foundation of the church will remain (But let the
stump and its roots), the church will be taken over by the pretenders of the bronze kingdom who mix their words with the
words of Jesus (bound with iron and bronze).

Then, Nebuchadnezzar provides the final details of the
dream:

> Let his mind be changed from that of a man and
> let him be given the mind of an animal, till seven
> times pass by for him. (Daniel 4:16)

We read that this punishment will last "seven times" and most think that this represents seven years, but is it practical to believe that it took this king seven years of living in the wilderness to get the message? Was the furnace really heated to "seven times hotter than usual?" We have no reason to believe that it took seven years for Nebuchadnezzar to understand this course correction and change his behavior accordingly. Like the furnace, the term *seven times* is used here to state that this time the punishment will be effective and complete—the king will convert to be the king that God decreed him to be. We know that this will be the end result—this is the event that will finally change the heart of Nebuchadnezzar to represent God's gold standard for rulers—Nebuchadnezzar will be the kingdom of gold.

The king continues to describe the vision:

> The decision is announced by messengers, the
> holy ones declare the verdict so that the living
> may know that the Most High is sovereign over
> all kingdoms on earth and gives them to anyone
> he wishes and sets over them the lowliest of
> people. (Daniel 4:17)

The angels have stated (is announced by messengers, the holy ones declare the verdict) so that all people will know (so that the living many know), Jesus (that the Most High) is above all kingdoms in the world (is sovereign over all kingdoms on earth) and selects anyone he wants to rule (and gives them to anyone he wishes and sets over them the lowliest of people). Nebuchadnezzar appears to humble himself in front of Daniel because all the pagans have failed at interpreting the dream and he has only Daniel left to rely on (Daniel 4:18). Nebuchadnezzar again reaffirms his pagan beliefs by telling Daniel that the "spirit of the holy gods is in you."

Daniel is reluctant to interpret the dream because he knows the news is bad and Daniel is afraid of Nebuchadnezzar's response:

> Then Daniel (also called Belteshazzar) was greatly perplexed for a time, and his thoughts terrified him. So the king said, "Belteshazzar, do not let the dream or its meaning alarm you." (Daniel 4:19)

Daniel knows that the Lord is about to punish this king and Daniel does not want to give the details of the wrath of God that will be poured out on Nebuchadnezzar for his rejection of God. The king reassures Daniel to give him the bad news without fear of reprisal. In response, Daniel starts out describing the tree as a beautiful and enormous one that protects and nourishes all who seek refuge in and under it—the tree of life (Daniel 4:20–21). Daniel then tells the king that:

> Your majesty, you are the tree! You have become great and strong; your greatness has grown until it reaches the sky and your dominion extends to distant parts of the earth. (Daniel 4:22)

Daniel describes how Nebuchadnezzar is the current leader chosen to represent God to the people he rules over. Daniel repeats the vision for Nebuchadnezzar without adding any details (Daniel 4:23), then starts explaining the interpretation as a punishment "decreed" by the God of heaven (Daniel 4:24).

Daniel informs the king that Nebuchadnezzar is not in charge—God is—and God is about to punish Nebuchadnezzar for his sinful ways:

> You will be driven away from people and will live with the wild animals; you will eat grass like the ox and be drenched with the dew of heaven. Seven times will pass by for you until you acknowledge that the Most High is sovereign over all kingdoms on earth and gives them to anyone he wishes. (Daniel 4:25)

God appoints the rulers of earth to rule as he pleases, and he removes a ruler at any time if he wishes. Again, we get the description of this "seven times" punishment that will be complete this time—it will change the king's heart in contrast to the other course corrections that did not have the same desired effect.

Daniel tells the king that his life will not be taken from him (Daniel 4:26), but then Daniel gives Nebuchadnezzar some advice:

> Therefore, Your Majesty, be pleased to accept my advice: Renounce your sins by doing what is right, and your wickedness by being kind to the

oppressed. It may be that then your prosperity will continue. (Daniel 4:27)

Daniel calls out the king for his sinning ways and tells him he needs to repent. Not only is God threatening to punish Nebuchadnezzar for his pagan ways, God wants this king to treat his subjects as God treats them—with love and kindness. Next, we learn that God provided Nebuchadnezzar some time to mull over what he has been told to see if his heart will change:

> All this happened to King Nebuchadnezzar. Twelve months later, as the king was walking on the roof of the royal palace of Babylon, he said, "Is not this the great Babylon I have built as the royal residence, by my mighty power and for the glory of majesty?" (Daniel 4:28–30)

God gave Nebuchadnezzar twelve months to change but rather than repent, this king became more arrogant than ever; he bragged about how powerful he was. Daniel's interpretation telling Nebuchadnezzar that God was going to punish him unless he repented and changed his ways had no effect.

God had enough:

> Even as the words were on his lips, a voice came from heaven, "This is what is decreed for you, King Nebuchadnezzar: Your royal authority has been taken away from you. You will be driven away from people and will live with the wild animals; you will eat grass like the ox. Seven times

will pass by for you until you acknowledge that
the Most High is sovereign over all kingdoms
on earth and given them to anyone he chooses.
(Daniel 4:31–32)

The words of arrogance immediately caused the king to
temporarily lose the rule of his kingdom. Nebuchadnezzar certainly connected his words to his punishment that was effective
immediately (Daniel 4:33). Daniel records that, "At the end of
that time, I, Nebuchadnezzar, raised my eyes to heaven, and my
sanity was restored" (Daniel 4:34). Did Nebuchadnezzar have
to eat grass and dwell aimlessly in the wild for seven years before he got the message? As we have already written, we can't
be certain, but we believe that the punishment was provided
until it was complete and the king's heart changed for good.

In closing this chapter, Nebuchadnezzar fully commits to the
Lord and praised God (Daniel 4:35–37). This last course correction finally converted this king to be the gold standard that God
had planned. Daniel doesn't tell us when Nebuchadnezzar had
this dream, but we can guess that God didn't wait too long after
he saw Nebuchadnezzar was not converted by Daniel's friends
surviving the hot furnace. We estimate the vision of the tree to
have happened a few years after the furnace event around 595
BC, and this means that God gave Nebuchadnezzar's his punishment twelve months later in 594 BC by banishing him to the
wilderness while losing his mind. We estimated the duration
of Nebuchadnezzar's punishment to be complete in two years,
therefore, Nebuchadnezzar became the gold standard with the
start of the kingdom of gold in 592 BC.

How many course corrections have you had that you ig-nored? This is a good time to reflect on your life and see if you have missed messages the Lord has attempted to give you. If you live in sin and have failed to repent, the Lord knows this because he sees and knows everything you do. If you are expe-riencing physical pain or mental anguish, it is likely the Lord telling you how unhappy he is with you. We know from his interaction with Nebuchadnezzar that the Lord will provide you painful course corrections to change your behavior. I can reflect on my life and remember my rejection of God and my ensuing punishment. If you are experiencing trouble and can't figure out why or how to solve it, maybe it's time you start look-ing internally rather than blaming your "bad luck" on others as we tend to sometimes do.

We wrap up the message of this vision with verses written a bit later by Daniel that verify the sins, punishment, and sincere repenting of Nebuchadnezzar:

> But when his heart became arrogant and hard-ened with pride, he was deposed from his royal throne and stripped of his glory. He was driven away from people and given the mind of an ani-mal; he lived with the wild donkeys and ate grass like the ox; and his body was drenched with the dew of heaven, until he acknowledged that the Most High God is sovereign over all kingdoms on earth and sets over them anyone he wishes. (Daniel 5:20–21)

Daniel wrote this and inserted it in the middle of a story of a king named Belshazzar who refused to repent and remained arrogant to God until the end. Nebuchadnezzar was a ruler who finally "got it" and understood that the only reason he was ruling was because God had allowed him to rule. By the time Daniel assembled his book, Daniel also "got it." Nebuchadnezzar as the gold standard was representing the promised Messiah in Daniel 9:24-27 – the tree of life.

Belshazzar, on the other hand, never got it. We will learn next the story of Belshazzar—an arrogant ruler that God removed because he failed to follow God. Nebuchadnezzar was punished for a time, then his punishment was complete—he repented and followed God until the end. Don't end up like Belshazzar, end up like Nebuchadnezzar—a king of gold.

We add the following to our time line:

Nebuchadnezzar's vision of a tree	595 BC
Nebuchadnezzar ignores God's rebuking for twelve months	594 BC
God temporarily removes Nebuchadnezzar's reign	594 BC
God restores Nebuchadnezzar's kingdom to him	592 BC
Nebuchadnezzar rules as a king following God	592-561 BC

CHAPTER 13

A Rebellious Ruler

ANIEL HAD STARTED OUT his new life in Babylonia with a boss that was a crazy, short-tempered ruler, then slowly over time helped transition this hotheaded king to one that followed the one true God. Daniel is the vessel that helped King Nebuchadnezzar take the right bus that transported him to meet Jesus—the subject of Nebuchadnezzar's visions. It was a tough journey like it is for many of us, but the connection was finally made, and King Nebuchadnezzar followed God until the end of his life. Daniel's story of Nebuchadnezzar was a good one, but as we presented earlier, after Nebuchadnezzar, the kingdom of God entered the inferior kingdom of silver when there would be some rulers who followed God and many others who rejected God. We are now in chapter five of Daniel discussing a ruler, Belshazzar, who rejected God—even though God sent him a direct warning to heed the course correction God provided him. God's warning to Belshazzar was ignored—in fact, it hardened the heart of the arrogant Belshazzar even more.

Looking at history, we see that there were other Babylonian rulers who apparently didn't follow God, sandwiched between Nebuchadnezzar and Belshazzar. Why is Daniel telling us about King Belshazzar when there have been at least four other kings before him who seemingly rejected God? I think there are three reasons for this, with the first and most important being

that God provided Daniel two very important visions during the reign of Belshazzar that he will capture later in his book. Second, Belshazzar is the last Babylonian king to rule and there will be a very important transition to the Persian kingdom that will be described at the end of chapter five in the book of Daniel. Third, Belshazzar was presented a very important course correction that God knew he would reject. The details of this provide evidence of God working in the lives of kings—some use the course corrections to convert to follow the one true God of heaven, but most are stubborn and will remain arrogant and reject God to the end of their life.

Daniel writes that after Nebuchadnezzar died, a descendent of Nebuchadnezzar named Belshazzar left the ways of his "father" to mock the Lord and worship idols:

> King Belshazzar gave a great banquet for a thousand of his nobles and drank wine with them. While Belshazzar was drinking his wine, he gave orders to bring in the gold and silver goblets that Nebuchadnezzar his father had taken from the temple in Jerusalem, so that the king and his nobles, his wives and his concubines might drink from them. So they brought in the gold goblets that had been taken from the temple of God in Jerusalem, and the king and his nobles, his wives and his concubines drank from them. As they drank the wine, they praised the gods of gold and silver, of bronze, iron, wood, and stone. (Daniel 5:1–4)

Using the gold and silver goblets taken from the temple in Jerusalem for use in a pagan party certainly would have gotten the attention of the Jews who would have seen this as an act of complete disobedience to God. This was a very arrogant move by King Belshazzar that demonstrated to those who surrounded him that Belshazzar thought he was invincible and could do whatever he wanted. According to history, this is now the fifth Babylonian ruler after Nebuchadnezzar and none of the previous ones did such an obvious demonstration of disdain for the Jews and their God. The kingdom has already seen big changes in rule—kings have left the dedication of the one true God of heaven in the past, and now the ruler is using items dedicated to the one true God of heaven to praise "the gods of gold and silver, bronze, iron, wood, and stone." These are not the materials of the statue as I initially considered they might be—they are the materials of idols.

God puts those in charge who he wants, and God had a message for Belshazzar:

> Suddenly the fingers of a human hand appeared and wrote on the plaster of the wall, near the lampstand in the royal palace. The king watched the hand as it wrote. (Daniel 5:5)

We know from Revelation that *lampstand* is a term for the church, and we also know that *church* is the connection between God and his people. Daniel might have been indicating here that the writing occurred at a location that the former king, Nebuchadnezzar, had used for worship, or this death sentence is written where Belshazzar is worshipping idols. A mysterious

hand of the Lord was giving this king a message (wrote on the plaster of the wall) about this king's connection to God (near the lampstand in the royal palace). Belshazzar must have connected this message mysteriously being written on the wall to his desecration of the temple items in pagan worship because he is terrified (Daniel 5:6). Rather than calling on Daniel, who is a wise man following the Lord, Belshazzar, like Nebuchadnezzar did many years before, summoned the pagans for assistance to interpret the writing on the wall (Daniel 5:7). As expected, we learn that the pagans were unable to interpret the writing on the wall (Daniel 5:8) and because of this Belshazzar became "even more terrified, his "face became even more pale," and his "nobles were baffled" (Daniel 5:9).

The queen attempted to calm Belshazzar down by telling him of his magnificence and pointing him to Daniel for help:

> The queen, hearing the voices of the king and his nobles, came into the banquet hall. "May the king live forever!" she said, "Don't be alarmed! Don't look so pale! There is a man in your kingdom who has the spirit of the holy gods in him." (Daniel 5:10)

The queen says a few things to try to calm down Belshazzar— "May the king live forever" and "Don't be alarmed!" While pointing Belshazzar to Daniel, the queen verifies her pagan beliefs (There is a man in your kingdom who has the spirit of the holy gods in him). The queen went on to attribute Daniel's talent of interpreting dreams to being one with the gods (Daniel

5:11–12), then Belshazzar summoned Daniel and promised him great rewards if he could solve the mystery (Daniel 5:13–16).

This time Daniel rejects the thought of getting rewards for following the Lord because he knows the heart of Belshazzar:

> Then Daniel answered the king, "You may keep your gifts for yourself and give your rewards to someone else. Nevertheless, I will read the writing for the king and tell him what it means. (Daniel 5:17)

The response of Daniel sounds like he is not a fan of Belshazzar because this king is not even pretending to follow the Lord. Daniel agrees to interpret the writing for this king (I will read the writing for the king and tell him what it means). First, Daniel recaps how the Lord blessed Nebuchadnezzar (Daniel 5:18–19), but Nebuchadnezzar remained arrogant and rejected God, so God punished him (Daniel 5:20–21). Daniel tells Belshazzar that the Lord also tried to convert this king, but Belshazzar has not humbled himself before the Lord as evidenced by the way he turned his back on the Lord by using the temple goblets in idol worship (Daniel 5:22–23). Not only was Belshazzar rejecting God, but he was mocking the Lord by using items from the temple in pagan worship that had been dedicated to the Lord.

Daniel reads the message the Lord wrote on the wall, and it is not a good message for this king. The Lord will use the Medes and Persians to forcibly remove Belshazzar and they will become the new rulers (Daniel 5:24–28). The words of the Lord do not frighten Belshazzar; in fact, it emboldens him as he again

mocks the Lord by rewarding Daniel for giving him the news that his kingdom will soon end:

> Then at Belshazzar's command, Daniel was clothed in purple, a gold chain was placed around his neck, and he was proclaimed the third-highest ruler in the kingdom. (Daniel 5:29)

This certainly reads like Belshazzar is mocking Daniel for stating that Belshazzar will be executed and replaced (was clothed in purple, and a gold chain was placed around his neck). Does Daniel seem like the kind of guy that would willingly have a gold chain placed around his neck? Not to me.

Then, as promised in the writing, the Lord punished Belshazzar and removed him from his throne:

> That very night Belshazzar, king of the Babylonians, was slain, and Darius the Mede took over the kingdom, at the age of sixty-two. (Daniel 5:30–31)

Belshazzar did not recognize his sin and repent of his ways to follow the God of heaven, so God punished him and replaced him with a king that would. God had the Persians execute and replace Belshazzar. We have already thoroughly addressed this verse to prove that Daniel 5:31 was either translated or copied in error, or Daniel miswrote it to state that Darius took over the rule when he really meant to state it was King Cyrus "at the age of sixty-two." When Cyrus took over, Daniel was the leader of the wise men (Daniel 1:21, 2:48) and, on that same day, is appointed by Belshazzar to the third-highest position in the kingdom (Daniel 5:28). The first year of Cyrus is the same as the last day of Belshazzar's reign, and although Daniel has pointed to this event as taking place in the first year of Darius, we know there has been a mistake. Daniel mistakenly noted that this transition was to Darius because the next subject Daniel presents fast-forwards seventeen years to 522 BC when Darius *is in charge.*

In closing, we confirm a few more details of the time line data we presented earlier:

Daniel is promoted to the third-highest ruler in the kingdom	539 BC
Daniel interprets the writing on the wall	539 BC
King Cyrus' reign begins	539 BC

CHAPTER 14

Unbreakable Decrees

CHAPTER SIX OF THE book of Daniel starts out presenting details that indicate Daniel was so admired by the new ruler King Darius, that Darius is about to appoint Daniel to be "over the whole kingdom." Right from the start of this event it appears as though Daniel has the confidence of the new Persian king Darius:

> It pleased Darius to appoint 120 satraps to rule throughout the kingdom, with three administrators over them, one of whom was Daniel. The satraps were made accountable to them so that the king might not suffer from loss. Now Daniel so distinguished himself among the administrators and the satraps by his exceptional qualities that the king planned to set him over the whole kingdom. (Daniel 6:1–3)

At the start of this event, Daniel has proven himself to be a great administrator to the Persians, therefore, King Darius has planned to put him in charge of the whole kingdom—Darius wants to appoint Daniel as the COO—Chief Operating Officer. History and the Bible tell us that this occurrence is taking place in 522 BC after Daniel has seventeen years of administrative management experience and, therefore, is about ninety-three

years old. Daniel has proven leadership qualities, including honesty and integrity, and the other managers reporting to Darius do not like these qualities. The other managers are corrupt and having Daniel in this position would put a dent in their benefits, so they schemed on how to get rid of Daniel.

The other administrators and satraps in Darius' kingdom were pagans so they determined the best way to get rid of Daniel was to use Daniel's dedication and worship of the one true God against him (Daniel 6:4–5). The corrupt leaders approached Darius and heaped empty praises on the king to persuade Darius to mandate that for the next thirty days anyone caught praising a god besides Darius would be thrown into the lion's den as punishment (Daniel 6:6–7). Notice that these leaders have proclaimed Darius to be a god, and because this proposal gains favor with Darius, we know that when Darius takes over the kingdom, he is a pagan ruler.

The next verses describe the unbreakable decrees of the Medes and Persians that are applied later to the promise of the Messiah—the decree of the seventy sevens (Daniel 9:24):

> Now, Your Majesty, issue the decree and put it in writing so that it cannot be altered—in accordance with the law of the Medes and Persians, which cannot be repealed. (Daniel 6:8)

Any decree by the king, per the laws of the Medes, "cannot be altered," therefore edicts were permanent. The evil managers trying to get rid of Daniel request Darius to permanently decree a law that will certainly result in Daniel's death. Daniel has jumped ahead seventeen years with this story of the lion's den and the permanent decrees of the Medes and Persians because the concept of a permanent decree is important to understand the rest of Daniel's book. Not only will an unbreakable decree be referenced for the promise of the Messiah (Daniel 9:24–27), it will also apply to the fulfillment of Jeremiah's prophecy of the seventy (Daniel 9:1–4) that captures the love of God for his people.

God's promises, like the decrees of the Medes and Persians, are permanent—they can never be altered or changed. We are about to see how a permanent decree of the Medes and Persians resulted in a death sentence for Daniel, but God spared Daniel from death with his permanent decree of salvation. Daniel followed the laws of God, and this put him in favor with God who saves from death the ones who love him. I hope you also see the connection to the decree of the Messiah. God promised his people that a Messiah would come who will permanently save the people from the decree of the death sentence from sin that we are all born with.

King Darius follows the advice of the evil men in his kingdom (Daniel 6:9); then, just like the three friends of Daniel who refused to worship pagan gods, suffered a death sentence, and survived, the same thing happens to Daniel. Daniel refused to obey this order that would have had Daniel turn from the one true God of heaven to worship something that is not God. Daniel was proud of his dedication to the Lord and wanted everyone to see his blatant rejection of the pagan ways of these other managers and the new ruler:

> Now when Daniel learned that the decree had
> been published, he went home to his upstairs

room where the windows opened toward Jerusalem. Three times a day he got down on his knees and prayed, giving thanks to his God, just as he had done before. (Daniel 6:10)

Daniel was a bold follower of the one true God of heaven; he was clearly a dedicated man of God and wanted everyone to see it. Daniel was firm in his beliefs and was not about to change and worship idols even if it meant the king would execute him.

Of course, the pagan managers felt victorious and went straight to the king to report Daniel for breaking his new decree of worship (Daniel 6:11–12). These evil men knew that Darius favored Daniel so they reinforced to the king that a law of the Medes and Persians cannot be altered, changed, or ignored. Darius confirmed that the laws of Persian rulers are permanent:

> The king answered, "The decree stands—in accordance with the law of the Medes and Persians, which cannot be repealed." (Daniel 6:12)

The corrupt men again reinforced to King Darius how Daniel refused to worship Darius as a god and had broken the decree (Daniel 6:13). Darius was saddened because he was fond of Daniel so he "made every effort" he could to try to save Daniel's life (Daniel 6:14). The corrupt leaders wanted Daniel out of the way, so they again reinforced the responsibilities of the king to follow the unbreakable law:

> Then the men went as a group to King Darius and said to him, "Remember, Your Majesty, that according to the law of the Medes and Persians

no decree or edict that the king issues can be changed." (Daniel 6:15)

This is now the third reference to the importance of the laws of the Medes and Persians; so, do you think this is an important message? Daniel reinforced the permanency of the decree of the Medes and Persians because, although he faced death, the Lord was about to save his life. In chapter nine of Daniel, another permanent decree is made during the reign of Darius—the seventy sevens revealed by an angel of God named Gabriel that came to Daniel in a vision. With the decree described in chapter nine, people will, like Daniel, have a death sentence but will survive death with the promise of eternal life.

Per the decree, Darius fulfilled the law and threw Daniel into the den of hungry lions:

> So the king gave the order, and they brought Daniel and threw him into the lion's den. The king said to Daniel, "May your God, who you serve continually, rescue you!" (Daniel 6:16)

From this verse we know that Darius has a soft heart for Daniel's God and admires the dedication that Daniel has to the Lord (The king said to Daniel, "May your God, who you serve continually, rescue you!"). We also see that Daniel *continually* worships God. This story is not only a story of redemption, it is also the documentation of God giving another Persian king a course correction to try to change the heart of a ruler to give up his pagan gods to worship the one true God of heaven. The next morning, Darius immediately went to the lion's den and called out for Daniel (Daniel 6:17–20) and Darius found him

alive (Daniel 6:21–22). The king had Daniel removed to find him untouched (Daniel 6:23). We then learn that King Darius punished those who had schemed to remove Daniel from his role as an administrator by having the corrupt men and their families thrown into the lion's den—of course God did not save the evil men from their death sentence (Daniel 6:24) like he saved Daniel.

This course correction was effective; Darius recognized the power of the one true God and changed from his pagan ways to worship Daniel's God. Darius witnessed how Daniel's *faith in God* spared his life and in response Darius professed his sincere faith in God:

> Then King Darius wrote to all the nations and peoples of every language in all the earth: "May you prosper greatly! I issue a decree that in every part of my kingdom people must fear and reverence the God of Daniel. For he is the living God and he endures forever, his kingdom will not be destroyed, his dominion will never end." (Daniel 6:25–26)

This experience proved the majesty of the one true living God who "endures forever" and "his kingdom will not be destroyed" and "never end." The decrees of the Persians are permanent; therefore, this statement will govern the people forever. You should also recognize the tie-in here to the kingdom of iron from the statue that will never end. Like this permanent decree recognizing the one true God of heaven as the only God, the iron kingdom of the statue that represents Jesus is a permanent kingdom that will never end.

We have seen a decree of death overcome by the power of a decree of life through the kingdom of God. God once decreed that all people through their sin will die, but now God has promised that if you follow God with your heart and soul, you will live. In addition, Darius witnessed how God's decree is over and above any decree made by men. The decree of death by Darius cannot be fulfilled when there is another decree by the one true God of heaven that saves life.

Finally, we then get that very important piece of scripture to end chapter six of the book of Daniel:

> So Daniel prospered during the reign of Darius
> and the reign of Cyrus the Persian. (Daniel 6:28)

There is only one reason for Daniel, this man that lived his life for God, to state the words that he "prospered" during the reign of kings Darius and Cyrus—these rulers followed the God of Daniel. God used course corrections together with Daniel to convert these two kings from pagan worshippers to rulers that followed the one true God of heaven. Darius was a bright guy who saw the power of the one true God after his first course correction. We don't know how many years Daniel lived during Darius' reign, and we don't know from the book of Daniel if Darius remained dedicated to God throughout his nearly thirty-six-year reign from 522 BC through 486 BC. But we do know that Darius followed God while Daniel was alive.

CHAPTER 15

Beasts Will Reign over the People of God

ANIEL HAD JUMPED AHEAD to the lion's den story during the kingdom of Darius in 522 BC to provide the story of God's wonderful promise for redemption from the death sentence we each have when we are born into this world. Now that we understand how God's permanent decree of life saved the lives of Daniel and his friends, Daniel will present a vision he had that provide additional details of the kingdom of God. The message that Daniel now provides through his vision has some not so good aspects, but it ends well. During the first year of the reign of the corrupt king Belshazzar, Daniel received a vision that focused on how people will corrupt the kingdom of God on earth.

First the introduction:

> In the first year of Belshazzar king of Babylon, Daniel had a dream, and visions passed through his mind as he was lying in bed. He wrote down the substance of his dream. (Daniel 7:1)

I already addressed this verse earlier because it helped me understand the visions I was receiving from the Holy Spirit. As I previously noted, for about the past three years I have been

waking up with visions that have provided me insight and direction about what scripture to investigate and these visions and messages have helped me interpret and document the results. Until I read this passage, I had trouble describing these visions to others and, when I tried, I usually received sarcastic feedback such as, "So you believe that God is talking to you?" I struggled with a response because yes, God is talking to me, but it's not what it sounds like. It isn't as though I'm standing somewhere with God talking to me. The Holy Spirit speaks to me as I'm in a semiawake state, then I lie there and ponder what I am being told. After a short while I rise to pray and start writing—just as Daniel described!

Daniel starts to document details of the vision he has just seen:

> Daniel said: "In my vision at night I looked, and
> there before me were the four winds of heaven
> churning up the great sea. (Daniel 7:2)

Four winds of heaven represents the spirit of God poured out on all people (Mark 13:27, Revelation 7:1) and *sea* is representative of the kingdom of God (Jeremiah 51:42)—the Holy City (Zachariah 14:8–9). There is trouble coming to the kingdom of God on earth—the church. Daniel is told that the kingdom of God, the church throughout the world, will be experiencing turmoil (churning up the great sea). Is this representative of Belshazzar's reign in the kingdom of silver with the inferior rulers that Daniel finds himself in, or is this a reference to something else? The answer is yes—to both. According to the statue, the kingdom of gold during Nebuchadnezzar's reign has ended and Daniel is currently in the kingdom of silver where there will be mostly rulers who do not follow God—they follow pagans. Belshazzar is one of those pagan rulers. Since Daniel is already in the kingdom of silver and there is a change coming to the kingdom of God on earth, this turmoil must be describing the transition to the kingdom of bronze—the God pretenders.

The description of the kingdom of bronze is not a good one:

> Four great beasts, each different from the others, came up out of the sea. (Daniel 7:3)

Throughout the Bible, *the beast* represents evil. The book of Revelation mentions the beast thirty-four times and there is one verse that clearly captures the meaning of the beast:

> The dragon gave the beast his power and his throne and great authority. (Revelation 13:2)

The term *dragon* is mentioned in the book of Revelation fourteen times, but is best defined by the following verse:

> Then war broke out in heaven. Michael and his angels fought against the dragon, and the dragon and his angels fought back. (Revelation 12:7)

The dragon is the devil who is fighting against the angels of God. Therefore, in summary, the beast is in the church working with the devil—we have four beasts indicating that they are coming from all four directions and covering the entire kingdom of God on earth. These beasts come from within the

church (came up out of the sea)—they will originate with false teachers or, rather, those pretending to follow God.

Daniel describes this entity of evil—beast by beast:

> The first was like a lion, and it had the wings of an eagle. I watched until its wings were torn off and it was lifted from the ground so that it stood on two feet like a human being, and the mind of a human was given to it. (Daniel 7:4)

Jesus is described in the book of Revelation as the "Lion of the tribe of Judah" (Revelation 5:5). This beast is *like a lion*, it is like Jesus, but it is not Jesus—it is from evil, therefore, it must be pretending to be Jesus. After I wrote this, I thought of a band in the 1980s named The Pretenders, but this vision is not about music—Daniel is seeing the transition in the kingdom of God to an evil entity that wants to play God—he is getting a detailed description of the kingdom of bronze—the "pretenders." This beast did not come from heaven to earth, die, then rise and ascend back to heaven, it had to be "lifted from the ground" to appear as though it did. It isn't spiritual (it stood on two feet like a human being); it is human (and the mind of a human was given to it). This beast also tries to appear majestic—it will act as though it can be everywhere (wings of an eagle) just like Jesus is. The characteristics of this beast match the bronze material of the statue—Jesus is the gold standard, and this beast tries to look and act like Jesus.

Then Daniel describes the second beast that appeared in his vision:

And there before me was a second beast, which looked like a bear. It was raised up on one of its sides, and it had three ribs in its mouth between its teeth. It was told, "Get up and eat your fill of flesh!" (Daniel 7:5)

This second beast is very menacing and powerful (looked like a bear). Again, it will want to appear like Jesus who rose from the dead, but it falls short of Jesus (it was raised up on one of its sides). This beast will undertake a violent attack on Jesus (three ribs in its mouth between its teeth) and will execute a designated number of people who have committed to follow Jesus (It was told, "Get up and eat your *fill* of flesh"). The analysis of the book of Revelation will show that the "fill of flesh" is set at 144,000 executions. Also, from Revelation you will learn that those who oppose the beast will be executed by the beast. We know from recorded history that the RCC will take over the church of Jesus Christ by pretending to be the spokespeople for Jesus. We exposed their fraud and deception in the previous book, *The Early Church Father Catholic Fraud*. Hmm . . . I've just made a connection of these beasts to the RCC and the beasts in Revelation . . . we will explore this aspect of Daniel in just a little bit.

The third beast looks like a leopard:

After that I looked, and there before me was another beast, one that looked like a leopard. And on its back it had four wings like those of a bird. This beast had four heads, and it was given authority to rule. (Daniel 7:6)

At the site http://www.lions.org/leopards/leopard-charac-teristics.html, I found a perfect description of a leopard that explained what Daniel was seeing:

> Although they are the smallest of the big cat species, leopards are still a powerful force to be reckoned with. In particular, their skulls are no-tably large, and their jaws are so powerful that they can take prey much larger than themselves. Their shoulder muscles are also particularly strong and give leopards their unique ability to climb trees often whilst carrying remarkably heavy kills. Leopards climb back down from trees headfirst.

The description of a beast as a leopard indicates that this evil entity will be fast, powerful, and a great vicious predator. The beast will swiftly grow to a powerful and mighty conqueror (like a leopard) that will quickly spread throughout the world (four wings like that of a bird). This beast will proclaim to be the unity of trinity of holiness in God, the Holy Spirit, and Jesus but it will also have the devil as a leader—it will have "four heads." God will allow this evil entity to reign over the church during the kingdom of bronze (it was given authority to rule).

It is time for the comparison to what John the Apostle of Jesus wrote in the book of Revelation:

> The dragon stood on the shore of the sea. And I saw a beast coming out of the sea. It had ten horns and seven heads, with ten crowns on its horns, and on each head a blasphemous name.

The beast I saw resembled a leopard, but had feet like those of a bear and a mouth like that of a lion. (Revelation 13:1–2)

Wow! I hope you got the message like I just did. The one beast described in these two passages from the book of Revelation (the beast I saw resembled a *leopard*, but had feet like those of a *bear* and a mouth like that of a *lion*) just met the description of the three beasts in Daniel's vision. The three beasts described in Daniel's revelation are *combined* into the one beast that is described in Revelation 13:1–2. See the following table for a complete comparison:

Table 2
Comparison of the RCC Beast

Daniel	Revelation	Significance
The first was like a lion, and it had the wings of an eagle. I watched until its wings were torn off and it was lifted from the ground so that it stood on two feet like a human being, and the mind of a human was given to it. (Daniel 7:4)	a mouth like that of a lion. (Revelation 13:2)	It will pretend to be like Jesus and will claim that it is God that has come to earth in the form of a man.

And there before me was a second beast, which looked like a bear. It was raised up on one of its sides, and it had three ribs in its mouth between its teeth. It was told, "Get up and eat your fill of flesh!" (Daniel 7:5)	feet like those of a bear (Revelation 13:2)	The bear is a great predator and an enormous force. It will destroy all those that get in its way.
After that I looked, and there before me was another beast, one that looked like a leopard. And on its back it had four wings like those of a bird. This beast had four heads, and it was given authority to rule. (Daniel 7:6)	The beast I saw resembled a leopard (Revelation 13:2)	The leopard is the fastest predator in the world and years ago were known throughout the world. They are known to be graceful and fast with fierce hunting skills. They are also cunning and sly—they sneak up on their prey.

We can be certain that Daniel's beast is the great organization of false teachers who we refer to as the RCC who took over the APC. They are aggressive, brutal, and spread their evil throughout the world with lightning speed. In the book of Daniel, their rule is called "the kingdom of bronze"—the pretenders working on behalf of the devil. We aren't going to ignore the horns as we will attempt to address them in just a bit.

There is another beast in both John's book of Revelation and in Daniel's vision. If John's revelation is going to be like Daniel's, then I'm guessing ahead that the fourth beast in Daniel will match up with the second beast that John describes as the leader of the RCC known as "the Pope":

> After that, in my vision at night I looked, and
> there before me was a fourth beast—terrifying
> and frightening and very powerful. It had large
> iron teeth; it crushed and devoured its victims
> and trampled underfoot whatever was left. It
> was different from all the former beasts, and it
> had ten horns. (Daniel 7:7)

Daniel has told us that this beast will not be like the other beasts, but it does have some of the same qualities; it is "terrifying and frightening and very powerful." The statue told us that *iron* represented the coming of Jesus, and this beast has "large iron teeth." The beast represents an entity that will say it is the Lord, but from its description we know that it behaves opposite of Jesus. Jesus brings peace and love, but this evil entity brings hatred, war, and violence (it crushed and devoured its victims and trampled underfoot what was left). Daniel sees this last beast as something that will force itself on people it calls "its victims," and nothing will stop it.

Just as we did for the other beasts, we provide a comparison of the beast we know as the Pope of the RCC—the fourth beast of Daniel and the second beast of Revelation:

Table 3

Comparison of the Last Beast

Daniel	Revelation	Significance
It was different from all the former beasts, and it had ten horns. (Daniel 7:7)	beast that was covered with blasphemous names and had seven heads and ten horns. (Revelation 17:3) Then I saw a second beast, coming out of the earth. It had two horns like a lamb, but it spoke like a dragon. (Revelation 13:11)	When I read about the ten horns of the beast, I think of the Ten Commandments. This great false church known to be evil has set itself up as the administrator and enforcer of the laws of God—the one true church with leadership they claim has been passed down from Peter through Jesus. They will break all the laws of God.
It had large iron teeth; it crushed and devoured its victims and trampled underfoot whatever was left. (Daniel 7:7)	It exercises all the authority of the first beast on its behalf, and made the earth and its inhabitants worship the first beast, (Revelation 13:12)	This beast will force (made the earth and its inhabitants) to worship the other beast—it will stop at nothing to obtain allegiance to this great false church.
This horn had eyes like the eyes of a human being and a mouth that spoke boastfully. (Daniel 7:8)	It had horns like a lamb, but it spoke like a dragon. (Revelation 13:11)	This beast tells the world that it is speaking for God and is a representative of Jesus, but it is not—it is really the devil in disguise.

As we proceed in Daniel, we get additional information about the horns:

> While I was thinking about the horns, there be-
> fore me was another horn, a little one, which
> came up among them; and three of the first

horns were uprooted before it. This horn had eyes like the eyes of a human being and a mouth that spoke boastfully. (Daniel 7:8)

As the leader of the RCC, the Pope lays down the law but their law is not the same as the Ten Commandments—some of the laws of God are not important enough to be enforced (three of the first horns were uprooted before it). The law of the Pope is not from God (This horn had eyes like the eyes of a human)—it is from a man who acts like he is God (and a mouth that spoke boastfully).

The kingdom of bronze will last for a long time, but God has decreed it to end:

> As I looked, thrones were set in place, and the Ancient of Days took his seat. His clothing was as white as snow; the hair on his head was white like wool. His throne was flaming with fire, and its wheels were all ablaze. A river of fire was flowing, coming out from before him. Thousands upon thousands attended him; ten thousand times ten thousand stood before him. The court was seated, and the books were opened. (Daniel 7:9–10)

Jesus, who is God and has all authority (Ancient of Days), takes his seat at his throne (took his seat) to rule over the church and sets it on fire for Jesus (flaming with fire, and its wheels were all ablaze). Jesus has come back to earth to rule over his church and the church will be on fire for Jesus. Jesus will return to reign with the 144,000 martyrs (thousands upon

thousands attended him) and they will successfully bring a multitude to salvation by sharing the true message of Jesus (ten thousand times ten thousand stood before him). All those who were deceived by the Pope and the RCC during their reign will be judged for their deeds (The court was seated, and the books were opened). How do we know that they will be judged for their deeds? Because there is only one book of life and there is another group of books that record everything that is said and done (Revelation 20:12). There are many who try to follow Jesus but are stuck with following the lies of the RCC because they control the church. These people will not have their names in the book of life. These people will be judged for their deeds.

As Jesus comes to reign there will be a change in the kingdom of God:

> Then I continued to watch because of the boastful words the horn was speaking. I kept looking until the beast was slain and its body destroyed and thrown into the blazing fire. (The other beasts had been stripped of their authority, but were allowed to live for a period of time.) (Daniel 7:11–12)

The RCC and the Pope continue to tell the world they are God (I continued to watch because of the boastful words the horn was speaking), but when Jesus returns to reign God removes the authority of the Pope to control the Word of God (I kept looking until the beast was slain and its body destroyed and thrown into the blazing fire). Jesus returned to reign and the Pope's authority was removed in AD 1330 as we have already calculated and stated. This does not mean that there will no longer be a pope; the Pope will continue to exist but without authority to rule over the church. The RCC will also continue to exist but now their leader, the Pope, will rule without authority (The other beasts had been stripped of their authority, but were allowed to live for a period of time). The thousand-year reign of Jesus that started in 1330 is the mixed kingdom of the iron/clay that continues to rule over the church until the time of the end. We are currently in the kingdom of iron/baked clay. If you question this, look around to see the numerous pretender churches among those that are truly following the Jesus of scripture alone.

After the kingdom of iron/clay ends in AD 2330, the eternal kingdom of Jesus will arrive:

> In my vision at night I looked, and there before me was one like a son of man, coming with the clouds of heaven. He approached the Ancient of Days and was led into his presence. He was given authority, glory, and sovereign power; all nations and people of every language worshipped him. His dominion is an everlasting dominion that will not pass aways, and his kingdom is one that will never be destroyed. (Daniel 7:13–14)

The kingdom on earth is destroyed when Jesus (was like a son of man) is ready to establish the eternal kingdom. But Daniel says it is "*like* a son of man," so how do we know this Jesus? Because he "is coming with the clouds of heaven" and approached God (the Ancient of Days) and "was led into his

presence." Not only that, there is only one person who will rule over all and be worshipped (He was given authority, glory, and sovereign power: all nations and people of every language worshipped him), and that is Jesus. The eternal church with Jesus will last forever (His dominion is an everlasting dominion) and, unlike all other kingdoms that previously existed, the eternal kingdom of Jesus will last forever and will not pass away (and his kingdom is one that will never be destroyed).

Daniel is troubled by what he saw and asks for an explanation:

> I, Daniel, was troubled in spirit, and the visions that passed through my mind disturbed me. I approached one of those standing there and asked him the meaning of all this. So he told me and gave me the interpretation of these things: (Daniel 7:15–16)

Daniel has seen a lot and not only is it confusing, it is also overwhelming. He obtains the first part of the explanation:

> "The four beasts are four kings that will rise from the earth. But the holy people of the Most High will receive the kingdom and will possess it forever—yes, for ever and ever. (Daniel 7:17–18)

No issue here—an angel explains the meaning of the vision to Daniel. Note that although the four beasts have been described as all different, the angel has grouped them here all together as one group of "kings." The beasts are an evil entity that will come up from the world (the four beasts) who will rule over the entire church (are four kings that will rise from the earth), but God has decreed that the followers of Jesus (But the holy people of the Most High) will eventually and forever own the church (and possess it forever).

Daniel still is not understanding and, in fact, he won't understand what the visions mean until he is ninety-three years old, but he remembers that the fourth beast was different from the other three beasts, so he asks for an explanation:

> Then I wanted to know the meaning of the fourth beast, which was different from all the others and most terrifying, with its iron teeth and bronze claws—the beast that crushed and devoured its victims and trampled underfoot whatever was left. I also wanted to know about the ten horns on its head and about the other horn that came up, before which three of them fell—the horn that looked more imposing than the others and that had eyes and a mouth that spoke boastfully. (Daniel 7:19–20)

Daniel adds a clarification of the vision of the beast with a detail he left off earlier (and bronze claws) —Do you think this is a hint to the connection to the kingdom of bronze? I do! This beast will not only use the words of Jesus to forcibly take control over the church (iron teeth) it will also use the authority of the Pope as the leader of the RCC—the pretender of God—to tear apart anyone who opposes his authority (bronze claws) and refuses to join the ranks of the RCC.

Daniel is provided details that confirm our interpretation:

> As I watched, this horn was waging war against the holy people and defeating them, until the Ancient of Days came and pronounced judgment in favor of the holy people of the Most High, and the time came when they possessed the kingdom. (Daniel 7:21–22)

In summary, the kingdom of gold ended with the death of Nebuchadnezzar and Daniel is now living in the inferior kingdom with kings that follow the Lord God of heaven and others who are pagans and follow their own gods. After the kingdom of silver ends with the coming of Jesus, the pretender kingdom of the RCC will take control over the church. In these last two verses, we learn that the RCC wages war against the people of God, but Jesus will come back to rule over the church (until the Ancient of Days came and pronounced judgment in favor of the holy people of the Most High). Jesus will rule over the mixed kingdom of iron/clay, then the time of the end will come when Jesus ushers in his eternal church (and the time came when they possessed the kingdom).

This vision focused on the corruption of the church, but it also presented the entire future of the decree of God of the New Covenant—the kingdom of God on earth will change over time, just like the woman of Revelation indicates, but God is ultimately in charge and has laid out this path for his church. God has decreed the complete details of the future of the covenant between the people and God, and it will not change or be altered. It has been set with times decreed for the changes and the rulers.

Daniel receives more details about the reign of the fourth beast he questioned:

> He gave me this explanation: The fourth beast is a fourth kingdom that will appear on earth. It will be different from all the other kingdoms and will devour the whole earth, trampling it down and crushing it. The ten horns are ten kings who will come from this kingdom. After them, another king will arise, different from the earlier ones: he will subdue three kings. (Daniel 7:23–24)

This vision confirmed the changes in the kingdom of God as presented in Nebuchadnezzar's vision of the statue. The fourth beast, the ruler over the bronze kingdom—the Pope, with authority over the RCC—could be considered as a different kingdom from AD 30–1330 from the last half after Jesus came to the earth as the iron. Under the rule of the Pope, the RCC will be a vicious organization that prosecutes and brutalizes all who do not succumb to their rule (It will be different from all the other kingdoms and will devour the whole earth, trampling it down and crushing it). It will have ten horns for ten kings indicating that it completely takes over the law—the Ten Commandments. The Pope will start out in charge of the law of the RCC (The ten horns are ten kings who will come from this kingdom), but soon after they make their move, the Pope will end up replacing the trinity of God (he will subdue three kings). This means that the Pope will leave some of the law in place, but the trinity —God, the Holy Spirit, and Jesus—will all be "subdued."

Daniel receives more details about this designated ruler who reigns over the RCC:

> He will speak against the Most High and oppress his holy people and try to change the set times and the laws. The holy people will be delivered into his hands for a time, times and half a time. (Daniel 7:25)

The Pope that claims to be God will speak for Jesus as though he is Jesus (He will speak against the Most High). The Pope will prevent followers of Jesus from worshipping Jesus (and oppress his holy people) and will claim to have the power of God (and try to change the set times and the laws) who is the only one who can change the set times. Finally, Daniel is told that God has set an exact time for the RCC and the Pope to rule over the church and it will not be forever (The holy people will be delivered into his hands for a time, times and half a time). *A time, times and half a time* indicates that the Pope and the RCC will rule for a time set by God then their reign will end as decreed by God. It will not be changed or altered—it was predicted to last from AD 30 to AD 1330 when John Wycliffe's birth ushers in the transition to the freedom of the gospel to be taught to everyone rather than being controlled by the RCC.

Jesus will return to earth to rule over the church and the beast known as the Pope will lose his power and authority:

> But the court will sit, and his power will be taken away and completely destroyed forever. Then the sovereignty, power, and greatness of all the kingdoms under heaven will be handed over to

the holy people of the Most High. His kingdom
will be an everlasting kingdom, and all rulers
will worship and obey him. (Daniel 7:26–27)

No longer will the people of the earth be forced to obtain the
words of Jesus through the Pope or the beast—the RCC—God
will take away the authority and power of the Pope (But the
court will sit, and his power will be taken away and completely
destroyed forever). Once the Pope's power and authority are
removed, the church will be handed to the followers of Jesus—
the APC started by the disciples will make a comeback (Then
the sovereignty, power, and greatness of all the kingdoms under heaven will be handed over to the holy people of the Most
High.). After the church returns to the rule of Jesus, he will
reign for a time then Jesus will usher in his eternal church to
rule forever (His kingdom will be an everlasting kingdom).
Once the eternal kingdom of Jesus is established, there will no
longer be anyone in the kingdom challenging the rule of Jesus
(and all rulers will worship and obey him).

Finally, to end the complete summary of the church, Daniel
is honest about the overwhelming amount of information he
has been shown:

This is the end of the matter, I, Daniel, was deeply troubled by my thoughts and my face turned
pale, but I kept the matter to myself. (Daniel
7:28)

Daniel was in shock, and who wouldn't be? As I keep going
through the interpretation of prophecy that the Lord has provided me, I too am shocked. The details that reveal the time of

the end and the accuracy of God's message about the future of the church is overwhelming.

Imagine Daniel who is living 2,600 years ago receiving this vision! I have already commented several times that, based on my visions and trying to understand them and the comments that Daniel made, he was not able to understand the message the Lord was delivering to him until the last year or two of his life. I don't think he ever understood the complete details of his visions because who would conceive of the RCC and their pope without looking at history to see the verification of it? Daniel tells us that he was overwhelmed and scared, but why was he scared? Because he knew the vision was from God and it was not about angels, butterflies, and wonderful things—it was about beasts taking over the kingdom of God—that much he likely figured out at the ripe old age of ninety-three.

When Daniel received this vision in the first year of Belshazzar, he had already seen evil throughout the Babylonian kingdom and the rule of pagan kings. Daniel had also witnessed God in action through the course corrections he had provided rulers to persuade kings to leave their pagan ways behind to follow the one true God of heaven. Only one king, Nebuchadnezzar, followed God and the rest thus far in Daniel's life had rejected God. Daniel had seen how much God cares for the people of the world, but the vision Daniel received was not about a future peaceful time—it was about evil fighting against God until the time of the end.

CHAPTER 16

Daniel's Second Vision—A Ram and a Goat

A FEW YEARS AFTER HIS first vision during the reign of Belshazzar, Daniel received another vision that would provide the same message as the first he received about the beasts. Daniel will get more details of trouble in the kingdom of God and, in addition, he will get more reassurances that God is in control. In summary, there will be changes to come in the kingdom of God on earth. First, the Messiah will come to the world; then, an evil entity will rule over the church during the kingdom of bronze. Evil will not be completely removed from the church while the kingdom of God exists on earth but, in the end, the eternal church will come to the world with the people of God in his presence.

First, Daniel provides us the year when he received his second vision:

> In the third year of Belshazzar's reign, I, Daniel, had a vision, after the one that had already appeared to me. (Daniel 8:1)

Daniel's second vision takes place just before the end of Belshazzar's reign. Daniel's second vision during the reign of

Belshazzar starts out with a description of the two covenants between God and his people:

> In my vision I saw myself in the citadel of Susa in the province of Elam; in the vision I was beside the Ulai Canal. I looked up, and there before me was a ram with two horns standing beside the canal, and the horns were long. One of the horns was longer than the other but grew up later. I watched the ram as it charged toward the west and the north and the south. No animal could stand against it, and none could rescue from its power. It did as it pleased and became great. (Daniel 8:2–4)

This vision has directional components that initially baffled me. Daniel is in the "citadel of Susa in the province of Elam" and "beside the Ulai Canal," then a ram charged toward three directions, "the west and the north and the south." I searched for the meaning of these locations as they applied to the covenants of God and the message he had for Daniel in previous scripture and came up empty and disappointed.

Then, the Holy Spirit recognized I needed help, so I received the following vision on April 3, 2022:

> I was in a house that wasn't mine and I wasn't supposed to be there. I didn't know where this house was and why I was there, but I was trying to figure it out. The house had an old console stereo that I had moved away from the wall. With the top of the old stereo console open I

tried to tune into a channel that would let me know where I was, but I was having trouble finding the channel that would tell me what city I was in. Just as I thought I had found the station that would tell me where I was, I looked up and saw a car in front of the house and realized that the owner of the house had arrived. My thoughts quickly turned to putting the furniture back to where it originally was and finding a way out of the house. I could see the owner through the living room window, and Karen, my wife, was outside distracting the owner of the house. I quickly realized that there was no way I would have enough time to put things back in order and leave. It was an impossible task, then the vision was over.

I thought, "This is really cool—the Holy Spirit is providing me visions to understand Daniel's visions, but, wow, what a weird vision! I broke into someone else's house and moved around the furniture as though the house was mine. This seemed to remind me of the beast taking over the church that Daniel saw in his last vision. The beast who was in the church rearranged the Word of God to make it point to them and allow them to reign. I get that, but what about me trying to find out where I'm while I'm in the house?

I had already spent numerous hours in prayer and study trying to figure out those first verses, and I think the Lord was telling me that the meaning would come to me as I went through the vision in detail. I started to go through these verses word

by word, and this vision of mine was spot on. I was already told that the vision is about the church (saw myself in the citadel of Susa) where the Word of God is being studied (I was beside the Ulai Canal). Furthermore, we know that Jesus is the Lamb of God, and a ram is a grownup lamb, therefore, the ram must represent the kingdom of God. God made two covenants with his people (I looked up, and there before me was a ram with two horns standing beside the canal) and both covenants will last a long time (and the horns were long). The New Covenant started later with the coming of Jesus but lasted longer (One of the horns was longer than the other but grew up later). This was spot on when evaluating the total years for the Old and New Covenants. The Old Covenant made with Abraham lasted about 2,000 years and later we found that the hour of Jesus, the New Covenant, will last for 2,300 years. They were both calculated as long, but the New Covenant is represented by the longer horn because it will be three hundred more years.

Thus far, the discussion is directed toward the longer horn which is symbolic of the New Covenant of Jesus through his church spreading the Word of God. Jesus initiated the New Covenant, then the disciples (I watched the ram) started the church and spread the Word of God and the church to the rest of the world (I watched the ram as it charged toward the west and the north and the south). The New Covenant *must* have started in the east and spread throughout the world. God protected the disciples and Jesus during the start-up of the church (No animal could stand against it, and none could rescue from its power.). For seven years, Jesus and the disciples were protected (It did as it pleased) and the church with the words of Jesus was popular among the people (became great).

Next, Daniel is provided the details of the church break-in:

> As I was thinking about this, suddenly a goat
> with a prominent horn between its eyes came
> from the west, crossing the whole earth without
> touching the ground. It came toward the two-
> horned ram I had seen standing beside the canal
> and charged at it in great rage. (Daniel 8:5–6)

Immediately, after the seven-year protection period of the church is lifted by God (As I was thinking about this, suddenly), a corrupt entity with a thirst for power (a goat with a prominent horn between its eyes) that is opposed to the church because it comes from the opposite direction (came from the west) will spread very fast throughout the kingdom of God on earth (crossing the whole earth without touching the ground). Their false message and messengers will have no respect for either covenant—Jesus or the law (It came toward the two-horned ram I had seen standing beside the canal). The thief, or "beast" as it was called in Daniel's previous vision, attacked Jesus with all its might (and charged at it in great rage). Remember that the church of Jesus Christ started in the east and the RCC came from the west, because this detail will be revisited later.

This powerful evil entity we earlier determined as the beast of the RCC with their pope will cause grave danger to the church of Jesus Christ:

> I saw it attack the ram furiously, striking the ram
> and shattering its two horns. The ram was pow-
> erless to stand against it; the goat knocked it to

the ground and trampled on it, and none could rescue the ram from its power. (Daniel 8:7)

The pretenders, the RCC of the kingdom of bronze, will not care about either covenant made with God—they are out to attack Jesus and the law he fulfilled (striking the ram and shattering its two horns). The RCC was intent on replacing the covenant of God with their own laws and there wasn't anything that anybody could do to stop them (The ram was powerless to stand against it). The RCC removed Jesus from the earth by force (the goat knocked it to the ground and trampled on it) and they grew so powerful that they were able to take complete control of the church (none could rescue the ram from its power).

The RCC organization continued to grow in power, but this evil entity will experience internal strife and dissent:

> The goat became very great, but at the height of
> its power the large horn was broken off, and in
> its place four prominent horns grew up toward
> the four winds of heaven. (Daniel 8:8)

At the height of their power, the RCC will have internal leadership issues and will split into factions (the large horn was broken off) but it will survive and continue to successfully spread (in its place four prominent horns grew up) throughout the church—the kingdom of God on earth (toward the four winds of heaven).

Daniel is then reminded of the fourth beast from his previous vision, the RCC leader called the "Pope":

> Out of one of them came another horn, which
> started small but grew in power to the south
> and to the east and toward the Beautiful Land.
> It grew until it reached the host of the heavens,
> and it threw some of the starry host down to
> the earth and trampled on them. It set itself up
> to be as great as the commander of the army of
> the Lord; it took away the daily sacrifice from
> the Lord, and his sanctuary was thrown down.
> (Daniel 8:9–11)

The concept of pope started out to be a near insignificant concept (out of one of them came another horn, which started small), but the pope will evolve into a great and powerful entity (but grew in power) who will make agreements with a regional government that is likely the Romans (to the south). This is likely a reference to the allegiance between the RCC and the Roman government that is called the "Edict of Thessalonica." This agreement gave the RCC unlimited power to forcibly take control of the church of Jesus Christ (and to the east and toward the Beautiful Land). In a later vision, there is a detailed spiritual battle between kings, and we now know who the participants of this battle will be. The east is the church of Jesus Christ and the followers of Jesus, the west is the originators of the RCC, and the south is the RCC alliance with governments to forcibly take over the church. The RCC and the Roman government that legalized the persecution of anyone not committing to their church/state alliance will grow very powerful (It set itself up to be a great as the commander of the army of the

Lord). Together they destroyed the church of Jesus Christ (his sanctuary was thrown down).

Then Jesus provides you a blunt summary of the beast of the RCC:

> Because of rebellion, the Lord's people and the daily sacrifice were given over to it. It prospered in everything it did, and truth was thrown to the ground. (Daniel 8:12)

I hope you read chapter eight thus far and stated, "Wow, God told Daniel what would happen to the church of Jesus Christ centuries before it took place." God called the work of the RCC a "rebellion" because they did not accept the message and teachings of Jesus. The RCC became very wealthy through their church takeover and we demonstrated that fact in our last book, *The Early Church Father Catholic Fraud*. The RCC took over the kingdom of God on earth, and it made them very wealthy and popular (it prospered in everything it did). Furthermore, the words of Jesus were thrown away and replaced by the words of the RCC (and the truth was thrown to the ground). The accuracy of the predictions of the future of the church presented in Daniel 8:1–12 are about as powerful a statement from God being able to foretell the future, besides of course the coming of Jesus, that you can witness.

Next, we get to the introduction to that very important line of scripture that formed the basis for the time line of the future of the church and of creation:

> Then I heard a holy one speaking, and another holy one said to him, "How long will it take for

the vision to be fulfilled—the vision concerning the daily sacrifice, the rebellion that caused desolation, the surrender of the sanctuary, and the trampling underfoot of the Lord's people? (Daniel 8:13)

There are four important events in this vision that we have already thoroughly addressed:

1. "the daily sacrifice" that was replaced by the sacrifice of Jesus in AD 30;
2. "the rebellion that caused desolation" indicating that the Jews hated Jesus and rejected him, also starting in AD 30;
3. "the surrender of the sanctuary" was written about by John as he was starting the church when he noted that the church is full of antichrists that are not following the disciples' teaching—none of them are following Jesus (1 John 2:18–19)—this also started in AD 30 at the beginning of the church; and,
4. "the trampling underfoot of the Lord's people" that will take place over the entire period of the New Covenant (AD 30 to the time of the end)— followers of Jesus will be persecuted until the end of the New Covenant.

With Daniel having a clear vision of the entire New Covenant here, there was only one unanswered question remaining— "How long will the church and people of God be under attack (How long will it take for the vision to be fulfilled)?"

Daniel hears one of the holy men provide the answer to the question of how long this will be:

He said to me, "It will take 2,300 evenings and mornings; then the sanctuary will be reconsecrated. (Daniel 8:14)

The answer is directed to Daniel rather than the holy man who asked the question. The Lord wants Daniel to know the answer. Remember that term *evenings and mornings* that we discussed earlier in this book and claimed that it would be the end of creation? I hope you see how it can mean nothing else when put into context with the rest of the scripture detailing this vision. The church was consecrated as holy when Jesus made his sacrifice, then it immediately was infiltrated by the evil entity Jesus refers to as the "synagogue of Satan" (Revelation 2:9, 3:9). Daniel has been shown the transition of the covenant from the Old to the New, then the vision provided the details of the corruption of the church until the arrival of the eternal church. At the end of the kingdom of God on earth, the church will transition to the eternal church. The church will be reconsecrated as holy again only when the eternal church arrives. Therefore, there is only one answer for this scripture—Daniel has received the years corresponding to the hour of Jesus; the New Covenant will last 2,300 years to be exact.

Daniel 8:14 is the statement that completes creation—it is a time stamp or "set time" that provides the limited time of creation. Let me repeat this for emphasis. The church was consecrated when Jesus replaced the sacrifice in AD 30, then it immediately become unholy through the infiltration of false teachers who hated Jesus and wanted the church for their own selfish desires. The church will remain unholy until Jesus establishes his eternal church (Revelation 21–22, and various references to it in Daniel). Daniel has just been told that this will take 2,300 years, therefore, the time of the end must be AD 2330 when the eternal church of Jesus Christ arrives.

You might ask, "Why has this been hidden for so many years?" I asked myself this question too. Although the answer is way above my paygrade, I will take the liberty of providing my thoughts—right or wrong. As we have already discussed several times, the two prophetic books, Daniel and Revelation, are so connected and intertwined that they cannot be understood separately. I think theologians have, in the past, failed to connect the prophecy in these two books. Revelation points to Daniel and vice versa; without investigating and considering both together, the meanings of both are lost. There is another theory that bounces around in my head that I will also present. Criminals do not want their deeds to be exposed and that goes for criminals inside and outside of the church. The RCC remains a very powerful organized portion of the church and many people associated with the RCC have a lot to lose if their power were to end. The connection of the visions of Daniel to the RCC are so obvious that maybe theologians in the past have *purposely* directed readers of Daniel to a future antichrist, tribulation, and rapture to prevent them from seeing the existing corruption in the church. If the seventy sevens is *not about Jesus,* wild stories can be created that avoid the discussion of the RCC as the beast. With the seventy sevens pointing straight to Jesus, theology changes directions to point to the existing evil present in the church.

Daniel's vision ends with him returning to where he was when it started:

> While I, Daniel, was watching the vision and trying to understand it, there before me stood one who looked like a man. And I heard a man's voice from the Ulai calling, "Gabriel, tell this man the meaning of the vision." As he came near the place where I was standing, I was terrified and fell prostrate. "Son of man," he said to me, "understand that the vision concerns the time of the end." . . . Then he touched me and raised me to my feet. (Daniel 8:15–18)

Although Daniel was shocked (terrified and fell prostrate), he was reassured that the ending is not a bad one—there will be life and a resurrection at the time of the end. Daniel was "terrified and fell prostrate" because of the news he had received, but then he is immediately raised (Then he touched me and raised me to my feet)! To me this seemed like another message of the life-saving grace of God and his Son the Messiah—but Daniel did yet understand this—he has yet to unravel his visions, events, and interpretations.

CHAPTER 17

"Official" Interpretation of the Ram and a Goat

INTENTIONALLY SEPARATED OUT THE "official" interpretation of this vision because there are some apparent contradictions with what we've already presented as an interpretation that will take a bit of time and space to explain. The remaining scripture in chapter eight of the book of Daniel presents the "official" interpretation of the scripture that came straight from the angel Gabriel visiting Daniel from heaven:

> He said, "I am going to tell you what will happen later in the time of wrath, because the vision concerns the appointed time of the end. (Daniel 8:19)

The explanation of this vision starts with Daniel being told that the time of the end of the end times has been determined in advance and it will not change (appointed time of the end). In addition, we learn that Daniel will receive additional details about a "time of wrath" that will come later in the time of the end. This is the first mention of God's wrath in Daniel and there are two others:

- Daniel prays and asks God to turn his wrath away from the Holy City (Daniel 9:16), and, in answer to that prayer Daniel received the prophecy of how the Messiah will come to save people from their sins (Daniel 9:24–27).
- The last mention of wrath (Daniel 11:36) confirms to Daniel that the beast will exist and prosper in the world until the time of the end when the wrath of God is completely poured out.

The wrath of God was poured out on people during the time of Daniel, and it will continue to pour out through time. The book of Revelation provides many more details of the time of the wrath of God, but you'll have to wait for that summary. God pours his wrath out in response to sin, and prophecy is a story of how God redeems people of their sin and part of God's response is in the form of his wrath being poured out when people are disobedient.

Daniel receives the following explanation that on the surface appears to contradict our interpretation:

> The two-horned ram that you saw represented
> the kings of Media and Persia. The shaggy goat is
> the king of Greece, and the large horn between
> its eyes is the first king. (Daniel 8:20–21)

I'm sure you looked at this description and thought, "This guy's interpretation of this vision of Daniel is crazy!" Initially, when I read verses 8:20–21, I had the same reaction and wondered if I was misunderstanding the signals from the Holy Spirit—but then I started looking closely at these last two verses. On the surface, the explanation Daniel receives appears to be a lot different than the interpretation we just provided; but, when we take a closer look, we see the differences crumble. The two-horned ram represented God and his two covenants with his people—the Old Covenant of the law of Abraham and the New Covenant of the sacrifice of Jesus. But Daniel is told that the ram represents the "kings of Media and Persia," so it appears as though there is a contradiction. However, there is an aspect of the laws of the kingdoms of the Medes and Persians that applies to the covenants of God with his people—they are permanent and cannot be altered or broken. Remember when I asked you to file those references to the "Medes and Persians" for a future discussion because they are important? We are there. Daniel's life was threatened because of the permanency of the laws of the Medes and Persians, and I explained that this also represented the permanent covenant of people with Jesus. Not only does it apply to Jesus, the description of the decrees of the Medes and Persians also applies to the law of the Old Covenant. The covenants or decrees that God made with his people are permanent, complete, and cannot be altered. We learned earlier how the RCC and the Pope unsuccessfully tried to alter the set times, but they could not change them because God made them set times—they were permanent decrees.

For emphasis, let's repeat those three references to the Medes and Persians:

> Now your majesty, issue the decree and put it in writing so that it cannot be altered—in accordance with the law of the Medes and Persians, which cannot be repealed. (Daniel 6:8)

The king answered, "The decree stands—in accordance with the law of the Medes and Persians, which cannot be repealed." (Daniel 6:12)

Then the men went as a group to King Darius and said to him, "Remember, Your Majesty, that according to the law of the Medes and Persians no decree or edict that the king issues can be changed." (Daniel 6:15)

Do you think the kings of Media and Persia represent a covenant that cannot be broken? I hope so, because Daniel told us this three times and we know the significance of the number three (the trinity of God, Peter's denial, Jesus' resurrection after three days, etc.). Daniel told us in verse 8:20 that the ram represented the "kings of Media and Persia" and the important aspect of this—they have a decree that cannot be broken or altered. The ram represents the covenants between God and his people that are set and will not be broken or altered. These covenants are *permanent*.

But what about the shaggy goat being the king of Greece? Does this make sense. I turned again to the Bible to search for answers and found the following:

As Jesus was going up to Jerusalem, he took the twelve disciples aside, and on the way he said to them, "Behold, we are going up to Jerusalem, and the Son of Man will be delivered to the chief priests and scribes, and they will condemn him to death, and will hand him over to the Gentiles

to mock, to scourge, and to crucify and the third
day he will be raised up." (Matthew 20:17–19)

The Jews are God's chosen people, and everyone else called
the "Gentiles" are not. But wait, we are looking for the reference
to "Greeks" and not "Gentiles," so we turn back to scripture.
The Wycliffe Bible translation from www.biblegateway.com,
does not mention either Gentile or Greek in Matthew 20:19,
it calls the non-Jews "heathen men." To further demonstrate
translation similarities between the reference to Greek and
Gentile, the WEB translation of the book of Romans contains
eighteen references to Gentiles and six references to Greeks
but the NIV has only one reference to Greeks and twenty-eight
references to the Gentiles. Romans 10:12 is a prime example
of the NIV referring to Gentiles and the WEB version replaces
the word *Gentile* with *Greek*. Based on this, I logically reasoned
that the reference in Daniel 8:21 to "The shaggy goat is the king
of Greece" must indicate that the goat is representative of people who are not with the Lord. Although the goat has the same
God, they are not with God—they do not embrace or follow the
covenants.

We can get further clarification of this from the words of
Jesus when he stated:

> And they will fall by the edge of the sword,
> and will be led captive into all the nations; and
> Jerusalem will be trampled underfoot by the
> Gentiles until the times of the Gentiles are ful-
> filled. (Luke 21:24)

Jesus stated that the Gentiles will trample on the people of God from the beginning of the church until the time of the end. How do we know that the time of the Gentiles will be fulfilled at the end? Because the wrath of God ends with the judgment of those who rejected the law and Jesus, then the eternal church arrives (Revelation 20:11–21:27). The "shaggy goat" as the "king of Greece" with the "large horn between its eyes" from Daniel 8:20–21 is representative of people who oppose God.

Daniel receives a summary of his visions next:

> The four horns that replaced the one that was broken off represent four kingdoms that will emerge from his nation but will not have the same power. (Daniel 8:22)

Even from the beginning of their takeover of the church, the RCC will have factions of leaders that do not entirely agree with the RCC leader—the Pope. The large horn is represented as the consolidated power of evil, but those leading the corruption in the church will have disagreements and these disagreements will cause the RCC to split into factions that will each create their own similar organization. After they split, the RCC will not yield the same power and authority as it did earlier. Note that the large horn is referred to as a "nation" because it is a consolidation of power in agreement with the Roman government. A time will come when the RCC alliance with the governments of the world will split into factions.

Then, there is a prediction in Daniel of a very powerful leader who will emerge in the false teachers near the end of their reign:

In the latter part of their reign, when rebels have become completely wicked, a fierce-looking king, a master of intrigue, will arise. He will become very strong but by his own power. He will cause astounding devastation and will succeed in whatever he does. He will destroy those who are mighty, the holy people. He will cause deceit to prosper, and he will consider himself superior. When they feel secure, he will destroy many and take his stand against the Prince of princes. Yet he will be destroyed, but not by human power. The vision of the evenings and mornings that has been given you is true, but seal up the vision, for it concerns the distant future. (Daniel 8:23–26)

We know that the reign of the RCC will end in AD 1330 with John Wycliffe's birth and, before this time, the position of the Pope is that of a mighty warrior. In the latter part of their reign, Daniel is told that the RCC pope (a fierce-looking king) will become especially violent (strong but by his own power) and stomp out all opposition (astounding devastation) on a march throughout the world to convert all people of the world to be Catholic (he will consider himself superior). I searched the Internet for "an especially cruel pope" and the results pointed me directly to a pope named Innocent III who, according to https://ucatholic.com/resources/list-of-the-popes-of-the-catholic-church/, was the one hundred seventy-seventh pope who reigned over the RCC from 1198 to 1216. This is certainly the latter part of the reign of the RCC pope's rule over the

church that lasted from AD 30 to 1330. The brief summary of the leadership of Innocent III seems to verify the Daniel 8:23–26 prophecy provided by one source, the Encyclopedia Britannica online:

> **Innocent III**, original name **Lothar of Segni**, Italian **Lotario di Segni**, (born 1160/61, Gavignano Castle, Campagna di Roma, Papal States [now in Italy]—died July 16, 1216, Perugia), the most significant pope of the Middle Ages. Elected pope on January 8, 1198, Innocent III reformed the Roman Curia, reestablished and expanded the pope's authority over the Papal States, worked tirelessly to launch Crusades to recover the Holy Land, combated heresy in Italy and southern France, shaped a powerful and original doctrine of papal power within the church and in secular affairs, and in 1215 presided over the fourth Lateran Council, which reformed many clerical and lay practices within the church.

Note the key words in this summary, *"worked tirelessly to launch crusades"* and *"combated heresy."* The *crusades* were battles the RCC took to control their territory and *heresy* is anything that counters the beliefs of the RCC. The RCC had an army to expand and protect their investment as those claiming to be God. If you have trouble with that comment, visit *The Early Church Father Catholic Fraud* where we prove the RCC claim that the Pope speaks for God and if he speaks for God he is claiming to be equal with God. In addition, Daniel has described the popes as "kings." You should not have any problem connecting a vision of a pope and Daniel considering them to look like kings. This ruler, Innocent III, must have been singled out by the Lord to ensure we understood how devastating some of the reigns of the popes would be and to verify where in history Daniel's prophecy was.

But God will end the reign of the popes when he sends Jesus back to earth to reign over the church for one thousand years (Yet he will be destroyed, but not by human power.). Then, the end time will wind down during Jesus' reign as decreed by God (The vision of the evenings and mornings that has been given you is true). Next, Daniel is told to seal up the vision (but seal up the vision, for it concerns the distant future) because in 539 BC, when he received this vision, Daniel wouldn't have a clue what it is all about. Daniel is told to seal this vision then, seventeen years later in 522 BC, this vision and the rest of Daniel's life will be unsealed, and he will understand everything.

So, what did Daniel do after he received this vision? He tells us:

> I, Daniel, was worn out and I lay exhausted for several days. Then I got up and went about the king's business. I was appalled by the vision, it was beyond my understanding. (Daniel 8:27)

This description doesn't sound like somebody who knew what the Holy Spirit was showing Daniel—it sounds like somebody who is overwhelmed with trying to figure it all out. Daniel was "worn out," "exhausted," and "appalled"; and, who

wouldn't be? That is why the angel told Daniel not to worry about it yet—you will get plenty of time to unravel the message; so, for now, seal it up and go on your way—continue doing the king's business.

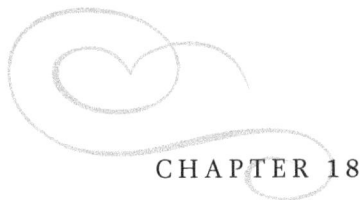

CHAPTER 18

The New Covenant Arrives!

W HAVE NOW APPROACHED chapter nine of the book of Daniel that contains the scripture God told Daniel was the most thorough and complete prophecy ever written. This prophecy of the Messiah contains a prediction of the exact year of the arrival of Jesus, along with the complete details of his mission. The mission of Jesus becomes crystal clear only through the prophecy of Daniel and Revelation combined. Since we already went through this prophecy in detail to provide the foundation for our analysis of the book of Daniel, we will not address that scripture again here other than to put it in into context with the rest of the message of Daniel's chapter nine. You will see how putting it into context ensures that the interpretation of Daniel 9:24–27 we have presented is accurate and provides the details of the fulfillment of Jeremiah's prophecy of the seventy.

As we enter chapter nine, we learn about the details of the vision Daniel received in the time of a Persian king named Darius:

> In the first year of Darius son of Xerxes (a Mede by descent), who was made ruler over the Babylonian kingdom—in the first year of his reign, I, Daniel, understood from the Scriptures, according to the word of the Lord given to

Jeremiah the prophet, that the desolation of Jerusalem would last seventy years. (Daniel 9:1–2)

We've already determined that this is near the end of Daniel's life and he is an old man, likely in his nineties by the time he receives this vision. First, we are told that Darius was *made* ruler over the Babylonian kingdom, therefore, we know that God had decreed this job for Darius prior to it happening. This points to the fulfilling of a verse in chapter eleven of Daniel that tells of an angel predicting the reign of Darius in advance (Daniel 10:20–11:1). There is another very interesting point to make about these passages—Daniel mentions twice that this is the first year of Darius. Why does he emphasize this? Because Daniel is now past the seventy years of God's promise to Jeremiah and Daniel is wondering what the heck is going on, because it appears as though God has not fulfilled his promise of redemption for the former kingdom of Israel. At the time of this vision, Daniel did not yet understand that God fulfilled Jeremiah's promise with a vision he received thirteen years before in the third year of Cyrus' reign.

To understand this second point, let's examine God's promise to Jeremiah:

> This whole land will be a desolation, and an astonishment; and these nations will serve the king of Babylon seventy years. "It will happen, when seventy years are accomplished, that I will punish the king of Babylon and that nation," (Jeremiah 25:11–12)

Most saw this as being a promise of redemption for Israel to go back and restore the physical kingdom of Israel; the "desolation of Jerusalem" was expected to last seventy years. Also, from scripture we learn:

> The land enjoyed it's sabbath rests; all the time of its desolation it rested, until the seventy years were completed in fulfillment of the word of the Lord spoken by Jeremiah. In the first year of Cyrus king of Persia, in order to fulfill the word of the Lord spoken by Jeremiah, the Lord moved the heart of Cyrus king of Persia to make a proclamation throughout his realm and also to put it in writing: This is what Cyrus king of Persia says: "The Lord, the God of heaven, has given me all the kingdoms of the earth and he has appointed me to build a temple for him at Jerusalem in Judah. Any of his people among you may go up, and may the Lord their God be with them." (2 Chronicles 36:21–23)

Nebuchadnezzar conquered Judah in 605 BC and, in the first year of Cyrus, 539 BC, a decree was made by this Persian king to rebuild the temple and restore the people of Israel to their land. However, nothing in the promise to Jeremiah indicates that the kingdom of Israel would be *restored* in seventy years. Nothing in that scripture from 2 Chronicles indicates that the kingdom of Israel is being restored either and that the Israelites would be a free people. Still, the Israelites believed that God made a promise that their kingdom would be restored in

seventy years—535 BC—and the proclamation by Cyrus for the people of Israel to return to their land was just the start. They believed that in four years from 539 BC the kingdom of Israel would be restored, but this has not happened. Daniel and the Israelites are in the first year of Darius in 522 BC—eighty-three years past Jeremiah's promise—and God has "made" another Persian king as ruler over the Israelites. Daniel has not seen the redemption of God's promise and is heartbroken.

This is not an easy period for the people of Israel as God continues to punish them for their sins and arrogant behavior. Daniel turns to the Lord in prayer for the current situation that the people of Israel still find themselves in (Daniel 9:3–19) and with that reference to the promise to Jeremiah, Daniel is looking for the answer. This prayer to God by Daniel in 522 BC indicates Daniel did not yet recognize that God fulfilled the promise made to Jeremiah though the vision Daniel received in the third year of Cyrus in 535 BC–presented in Daniel 10:1–12:13. First, Daniel states that he pleads for an answer and prays to the Lord (Daniel 9:3–4) with a confession of the sins of the Israelites; Daniel admits that the people have been disobedient to God (Daniel 9:5–6). Then Daniel tells God of the shame the people of Israel have faced because of their unfaithfulness and sin (Daniel 9:7–8). He reminds God of his past mercy and grace for the sins of the Israelites because they have not continually kept the law nor listened to the prophets (Daniel 9:9–11). Daniel continues his prayer by telling God that the predictions of a great disaster to befall on the Israelites has been fulfilled and the punishment was justified (Daniel 9:12–16).

Then, Daniel reminds God of the promise to Jeremiah:

Now, our God, hear the prayers and petitions of your servant. For your sake, Lord, look with favor on your desolate sanctuary. Give ear, our God, and hear; open your eyes and see the desolation of the city that bears your Name. We do not make requests of you because we are righteous, but because of your great mercy. Lord, listen! Lord, forgive! Lord, hear and act! For your sake, my God, do not delay, because your city and your people bear your Name. (Daniel 9:17–19)

Daniel is desperate for an answer to Jeremiah's prophecy for the restoration of the kingdom of Israel that would ultimately free the people of Israel from the reign of pagan foreign rulers. Daniel is begging God to hear Daniel's pleas, observe that the desolation of Jerusalem has not changed, and asks God to no longer delay the fulfillment of the promise God made to the people of Israel and recorded by the prophet Jeremiah. In response, Daniel receives a visit from an angel he has seen previously:

While I was speaking and praying, confessing my sin and the sin of my people Israel and making my request of the Lord my God for his holy hill—while I was still in prayer, Gabriel, the man I had seen in the earlier vision, came to me in swift flight about the time of the evening sacrifice. He instructed me and said to me, "Daniel,

I have now come to give you insight and understanding." (Daniel 9:20–22)

As I read this, I realized that there were two ways to interpret Gabriel's message as it is described:

1. Gabriel might have physically arrived *"about the time* of
   the daily sacrifice," in other words, Gabriel appeared at
   the normal time of the sacrifice; or,
2. Daniel just described the *purpose* of the visit—Gabriel
   arrived to present a message "about the *time* of the daily
   sacrifice," meaning that in the future there will come a
   time when the requirements of the daily sacrifice will
   change.

Gabriel's visit was about the coming of Jesus—the replacement sacrifice—therefore, there is no question that the second
option is the right one. Prior to moving on, I wondered if there
was a *set time* for the daily sacrifice. I searched for "what time
was the daily sacrifice required" and found no scripture to provide me any details of a specific time for the daily sacrifice; the
time of the daily sacrifice apparently was not important. Since
we know that this vision will provide Daniel *all* the details
about the coming Messiah, you can be certain that the meaning
of Daniel 9:20–22 is that Daniel will be receiving a summary
about the replacement of the sacrifice that will be the future of
redemption, and this vision has *no reference* to the *time* of the
daily sacrifice.

If you have a red marker and you are interested in the book
of Daniel, you would be wise to mark up the following piece
of scripture in Daniel 9:22: *"Daniel, I have now come to give you*

insight and understanding." The angel Gabriel is going to unseal the visions that Daniel has had so that he will gain "insight *and* understanding." It is now 522 BC and God is finally going to open the mind of Daniel so that, in a flash, he will *get* everything! The message that Daniel is about to receive will clear everything up for him—all his visions, events, and interpretations will come together in a sweet package he has been asked to document in a book we now refer to as the book of Daniel. Looking back in time, Daniel will see how Jeremiah's prophecy was fulfilled when Daniel received that vision in the third year of Cyrus' reign in 535 BC—seventy years after Jerusalem was overthrown and was made desolate. God had already provided Daniel an answer to Jeremiah's prophecy through several visions and events that Daniel needs to assemble.

There is one more introductory verse to that great section of prophecy that we haven't yet discussed:

> As soon as you began to pray, a word went out, which I have come to tell you, for you are highly esteemed. Therefore, consider the word and understand the vision. (Daniel 9:23)

Why did Daniel receive this message? Because not only is there a message for Daniel in this verse, but there is also a very important message for all of us in Daniel 9:23. God considered Daniel "highly esteemed" because of the sincere prayers of Daniel. God heard Daniel's prayers and sent an angel to answer them. Similarly, when you pray, God hears them immediately and takes them seriously. Your prayers, if they are sincere, are heard by the Lord and not only does God hear your prayers

he answers them. How many times has God answered your prayers and you haven't taken the time to understand the answer? I know in my life this has happened numerous times.

After the angel Gabriel told Daniel that he was there to provide Daniel "insight and understanding," he told Daniel to "consider the word and understand the vision." Gabriel emphasized that Daniel was to very carefully consider the words that he was about to be told because if he does, the light bulb will come on and Daniel will understand everything. We have already covered the promise made to Daniel through our long and detailed analysis of the seventy sevens. If you are having trouble putting Daniel's life of visions, course corrections, and how the Lord helped him understand the message he was to document in his book, I suggest you reread the earlier chapters and reexamine the prophecy of the seventy sevens.

CHAPTER 19

Jeremiah Will Be
Fulfilled . . . .

*Y*ES, AS THE TITLE claims, Jeremiah's vision will be fulfilled . . . just not in the ways the Israelites thought it would be. There are still people waiting and watching for the kingdom of Israel to be restored, but they have missed the message. This vision—the final one Daniel provided in his book—was received in the third year of Cyrus that is 535 BC—seventy years after Israel was invaded and taken captive by the Babylonians. I know that Cyrus took over the kingdom in 539 BC and this seems like 535 BC may be the fourth year of Cyrus, but we know that this scripture is correct, and the timing *must* work out so that 535 BC *was* considered by Daniel to be the third year of Cyrus—seventy years after the kingdom of Israel was overthrown with Jerusalem made desolate by the Babylonians. How can we be so sure?

We know that God decreed everything that is happening in advance—you noticed this when we assembled the messages earlier in this book that pinpointed the exact timing of the coming Messiah and his mission, and the length of times of the split New Covenant. God fulfills promises so we know that *exactly* seventy years after Jeremiah's promise, God fulfilled it. And how does Daniel's vision address Jeremiah's promise? By providing the complete future of the redemption of the people

of God. In this vision, God explained to Daniel how the sins of people will be forgiven through an unbreakable and permanent decree of God—a promise of eternal life through the Messiah. This vision contains the *complete future* of the kingdom of God on earth that God will use to educate people and draw them near to him. The future of the spiritual battle for the rest of the Old Covenant will be revealed, then the transition will be made to the New Covenant, then the future of the church of Jesus Christ will be presented with its replacement at the time of the end by the eternal church.

First, Daniel puts this vision into context:

> In the third year of Cyrus king of Persia, a revelation was given to Daniel (who was called Belshazzar). Its message was true and it concerned a great war. The understanding of the message came to him in a vision. (Daniel 10:1)

As stated already several times, Daniel received this vision in 535 BC—the third year of Cyrus' reign —seventy years after Jerusalem was overthrown by the Babylonians and Daniel was taken captive. Daniel reminds readers that he was given the pagan name Belshazzar because the Israelites are now ruled by pagan rulers. As Daniel recaptures this vision in his book, he now understands the meaning of it, because he included it last—it is the complete prophecy of the kingdom of God on earth that is from God and known to be true and addresses a great spiritual battle between pagan worshippers and those following the one true God of heaven. As Daniel writes this summary, he finally understands that the details of this ongoing spiritual war were revealed to him in this vision (The understanding of the message came to him in a vision).

Second, Daniel wants us all to know more about what led up to this vision:

> At that time, I Daniel, mourned for three weeks.
> I ate no choice food, no meat or wine touched
> my lips, and I used no lotion at all until the three
> weeks were over. (Daniel 10:2–3)

Why is Daniel mourning? This is obvious—Daniel is mourning because the seventy years have passed, and Jeremiah's promise has yet to be fulfilled. Then, Daniel starts to receive a vision:

> On the twenty-fourth day of the first month,
> as I was standing on the back of the great river,
> the Tigris, I looked up and there before me was
> a man dressed in linen, with a belt of fine gold
> from Uphaz around his waist. (Daniel 10:4–5)

The Tigris River was one of four rivers that watered the tree of life in the Garden of Eden (Genesis 2:8–14) and fine gold from Uphaz comes from the source where gold is mined (Jeremiah 10:9). In this vision Daniel has been transported to God's kingdom in heaven and there is a representative of God present.

Daniel obtains more details of this person in the vision:

> His body was like topaz, his face like lightning,
> his eyes like flaming torches, his arms and legs

like the gleam of burnished bronze, and his voice
like the sound of a multitude. (Daniel 10:6)

We get more details of the man, and the description is certainly one who appears to be representing God (his face like lightning, his eyes like flaming torches)—that is until you get to the arms and legs when it loses its majestic look (his arms and legs like the gleam of burnished bronze). Bronze is the material of the pretender kingdom of the statue; the man is not Jesus, but this man is speaking for the Lord (like the sound of a multitude). Daniel is the only one who sees the vision and his friends who were with him get scared and desert him (Daniel 10:7). Daniel is so overwhelmed that he fell to the ground in desperation (Daniel 10:8–9). The messenger reassures Daniel that his prayers are being heard by God and asks Daniel to carefully consider what he will be shown and told (Daniel 10:10–11). The messenger says he has come in response to Daniel's sincere prayers (Daniel 10:12)—Daniel is going to receive the details of how Jeremiah's promise will be fulfilled.

Then, Daniel obtains more details of this angel's visit:

> But the prince of the Persian kingdom resisted
> me twenty-one days. Then Michael, one of the
> chief princes, came to help me, because I was
> detained there with the king of Persia. Now I
> have come to explain to you what will happen
> to your people in the future, for the vision concerns a time yet to come. (Daniel 10:13–14)

The angels of God have been busy in this spiritual war trying to convert the heart of the Persian ruler who God has decreed will turn to God but has been stubborn and resisted (but the Persian kingdom resisted me twenty-one days). We learn that Daniel is not alone in this battle—there is an additional angel of God working on the heart of Cyrus (Then Michael, one of the chief princes, came to help me, because I was detained there with the king of Persia). We can conclude that the angels were successful changing the heart of Cyrus because the angels were no longer detained with the king of Persia and Daniel prospered during Cyrus reign (Daniel 6:28). Daniel has just been told about the spiritual war that was underway with Cyrus, and now the angel will tell Daniel about the future spiritual battle (Now I have come to explain to you what will happen to your people in the future). Daniel has just been bluntly told that this vision is an answer to Jeremiah's promise—Daniel will be provided the details of the promise of God to redeem his people.

Daniel is shocked to be getting this message and fell to the ground (Daniel 10:15). Daniel, who is troubled by the vision thus far, humbles himself before the man who we saw earlier was representing the Lord (Daniel 10:16–17) and the man comforts Daniel (Daniel 10:18–19). Daniel then starts to hear about the future:

> So he said, "Do you know why I have come to you? Soon I will return to fight against the prince of Persia, and when I go the prince of Greece will come; but first I will tell you what is written in the Book of Truth. (No one supports me against them except Michael, your prince. And in the first year of Darius the Mede, I took my stand to support and protect him.)." (Daniel 10:20–11:1)

The angels who are fighting for the Persian ruler will soon return to fight against the Persian rulers. We know that there are two Persian rulers between Cyrus and Darius that Daniel did not prosper under (Cambyses II and Bardiya) and we can assume that these are the Persian rulers who the angels will be fighting against. After fighting these two Persian rulers, the angels of God will be fighting against the Greeks, but before the Greeks come there will be one final Persian ruler named Darius who will be with God—at least in the first year of his reign. I hope you just picked up on the message of this verse—Daniel has been told that there will be a future ruler named Darius who will be with the Lord and the first year of Darius will be very important! Remember, we claimed that Darius was "made ruler" (Daniel 9:1)? Daniel wrote it that way because God had decreed it in this vision that told Daniel about Darius in advance.

Daniel receives additional details about the future:

> Now then, I tell you the truth: Three more kings will arise in Persia, and then a fourth, who will be far richer than all the others. When he has gained power by his wealth, he will stir up everyone against the kingdom of Greece. (Daniel 11:2)

Daniel is told that after Darius will come four more Persian rulers (three more kings will arise in Persia, and then a fourth). We did a brief search for Persian rulers and found at the site, https://www.thecollector.com/kings-of-persia/, a summary by Robert C. L. Holmes, that provided the following:

Xerxes I (485–465 BC)

Artaxerxes I (465–424 BC)

Darius II (424–404 BC)

Artaxerxes II (404–358 BC)

Robert Holmes presented the following summary for Artexerxes II that seems to verify the prophecy of the Greeks (He will stir up everyone against the kingdom of Greece):

> Shortly after the death of his father Arsaces, now as King of Persia Artaxerxes II, faced a rebellion led by his younger brother Cyrus who had risen to great fame while campaigning in Asia Minor. Cyrus led a large army bolstered by 10,000 Greek mercenaries, including the historian Xenophon who left an account of the expedition, against his brother. The King of Persia, despite initially hoping to resolve the conflict peacefully, emerged victorious.

In summary, afterwards Daniel receives details of the spiritual battle of the future from the messenger and recorded them in verses 11:3–12:4 and I summarize our path forward to analyze this scripture in the following bullets:

- There are many details in Daniel 11:3–12:4 that theologians have attempted to correlate with history.
- From Daniel 11:5–22 historians are confident in their correlation with scripture to past historical events.
- Theologians have spent countless hours trying to correlate this scripture to historical records but even their

attempts are uncertain. For example, when I read theological interpretations of Daniel 11:23–30 presented in the NIV, I see the word *either,* indicating theological uncertainty. From the NIV we obtain the following explanations:

> 11:22 *prince of the covenant.* Either the high priest Onias III, who was murdered in 170 BC, or, if the Hebrew for this phrase is translated "confederate prince," Ptolemy VI Philometor (181–146) of Egypt.

> 11:24 *richest provinces,* Either of the Holy Land or of Egypt. *Fortresses. In Egypt.*

- The interpretation of Daniel 11:31 falls off a cliff from what the Holy Spirit has been guiding me to. Theologians commonly describe the seventy sevens phrase *"abomination that causes desolation"* to refer to a pig roast on the altar of the temple to a pagan god in 168 BC, rather than pointing straight to Jesus as we have found.
- With the known date of the abomination that causes desolation occurring in AD 30 and assuming that Daniel 11:2 is a reference to Artaxerxes II who reigned until 358 BC, we know that Daniel 11:3–30 covers the years from 358 BC through AD 30.
- The messenger told Daniel up front that the message of this vision "was true and it concerned a great war," therefore, we know these verses accurately depict the future of the ongoing spiritual battle between the good of God and the evil choices that humans make.

I could attempt to go through each verse here and correlate it to history, but I failed to see the benefit of meticulously going through history to prove all these details were accurate. From what God predicted in Daniel that we have obviously seen fulfilled, we know that Daniel's visions are true prophecy from God.

With this knowledge, there is no benefit to me spending countless hours searching through and trying to connect each verse to an ongoing spiritual war. From past scripture we are told that Jesus and the church came out of the east and spread to the world as an evil entity from the west who joined forces with the Roman government in the south to attack and take over the church. I leave this subject here and move on to the verse just before Daniel 11:30 corresponding to the sacrifice of Jesus.

Starting with the verses just before the famous statement of "the abomination that causes desolation," we have:

> At the appointed time, he will invade the South again, but this time it is different from what it was before. Ships of the western coastlands will oppose him, and he will lose heart. Then he will turn back and vent his fury against the holy covenants. He will return and show favor to those who forsake the holy covenant. (Daniel 11:29–30)

Daniel has been receiving details of the ongoing spiritual war. The originators of the RCC will oppose the devil (Ships of the western coastlands will oppose him, and he will lose heart).

But it will not last —the devil will focus on destroying the transition of the Old Covenant to the New Covenant (he will turn back and vent his fury against the holy covenants). The false teachers will join with the devil to try to destroy Jesus even before the church is started. This sounds like the attempts of Herod to kill Jesus by a decree of death (Matthew 2:1–18) to prevent the one-time sacrifice of Jesus. Two of the many websites that can be a starting point for those interested in connecting the dots of Daniel to history are https://bnugent.org/the-roman-occupation-of-israel-and-the-messiahs-enigmatic-response/ and https://www.britannica.com/biography/Herod-king-of-Judaea. Pompey ruled over Jerusalem prior to the coming of Jesus and Herod ruled when Jesus was born. Both these men, Pompey and Herod, represent a Roman government who ruled over the people of Israel during the time of the coming of Jesus and hated the covenant of God with the Jews. I saw the details in these resources potentially leading to resolution but, again, I leave it to others.

Next, we have the famous "abomination that causes desolation" verse:

> His armed forces will rise up to desecrate the temple fortress and will abolish the daily sacrifice. Then they will set up the abomination that causes desolation. With flattery he will corrupt those who have violated the covenant, but the people who know their God will firmly resist him. (Daniel 11:30–32)

The devil together with the Roman rulers and false teachers will join forces to persecute Jesus (His armed forces will rise up to desecrate the temple fortress) and they will successfully execute Jesus as the sacrifice to replace the daily sacrifices (and will abolish the daily sacrifice). With their act of executing Jesus, the Jews and Roman government replaced the altar with the sacrifice of Jesus (they will set up the abomination). The Jews want nothing to do with the sacrifice of Jesus, so they vacate the new church of Jesus Christ (that causes desolation). They will join forces to attack the followers of Jesus and the new church (With flattery he will corrupt those who have violated the covenant) but true followers of Jesus will fight on behalf of the truth of scripture (but the people who know their God will firmly resist him). We get the term "he will corrupt" as a direct reference to the devil—if you recall, the RCC is working with the devil to take over the church; therefore, the devil, *he,* is an integral part of the spiritual battle.

Then, we get to the future of the church—the reign of the beast that arrives immediately after the sacrifice of Jesus:

> Those who are wise will instruct many, though for a time they will fall by the sword or be burned or captured or plundered. When they fall, they will receive a little help, and many who are not sincere will join them. Some of the wise will stumble, so that they may be refined, purified, and made spotless until the time of the end, for it will still come at the appointed time. (Daniel 11:33–35)

The disciples of Jesus and their followers who are true to the Word of God will spread the word (Those who are wise will instruct many), but after the three-and-a-half-year start of the church they will be persecuted and even killed (though for a time they will fall by the sword or be burned or captured or plundered). The church has become the corrupt RCC and some of those in the RCC will pledge allegiance to the RCC, but they do not believe their words (When they fall, they will receive a little help, and many who are not sincere will join them). Some in the RCC (Some of the wise will stumble) will reject the beast and follow Jesus (so that they may be refined, purified, and made spotless). We learned earlier that the RCC will try to change the set times, but they won't be able to because the time of the end of their reign will come as decreed by God (until the time of the end, for it will still come at the appointed time).

We obtain verification of the fourth beast of Daniel—the leader of the RCC—the Pope:

> "The king will do as he pleases. He will exalt and magnify himself above every god and will say unheard-of things against the God of gods. He will be successful until the time of wrath is completed, for what has been determined must take place. (Daniel 11:36)

The RCC and their pope (The king) will ignore Jesus to run the church as they wish (will do as he pleases). As we know from earlier, the RCC will proclaim the Pope to be God (He will exalt and magnify himself above every god) and while the Pope is pretending to be God, he will make claims that contradict the words of Jesus (and will say unheard-of things against the God of gods). Although the authority of the Pope will be removed when Jesus comes back to earth to rule, the position of the Pope will remain as a wealthy and popular spokesman for the RCC (He will be successful) until the time of the end (until the time of wrath is completed). This will all take place as decreed by God in the Books of Truth (for what has been determined must take place).

The RCC kingdom of bronze will focus on wealth, prosperity, and self-gratification instead of being dedicated solely to Jesus:

> He will show no regard for the gods of his ances-
> tors or for the one desired by women, nor will
> he regard any god, but will exalt himself above
> them all. Instead of them, he will honor a god
> of fortresses; a god unknown to his ancestors he
> will honor with gold and silver, with precious
> stones and costly gifts. (Daniel 11:37–38)

First, who would be the "one desired by women?" In the book of Revelation, a woman represents the church of Jesus Christ and how it changes. The arrogance of the RCC is so great that they will put themselves above every other false teacher (He will show no regard for the gods of his ancestors), above the true church of Jesus Christ—the APC (or for the one desired by woman) and the Pope will declare he is God (but will exalt himself above them all). The RCC will build themselves a dynasty of buildings and property consisting of the Vatican and churches throughout the world (Instead of them, he will honor

a god of fortresses) and the RCC will become very wealthy (with gold and silver, with precious stones and costly gifts).

The description of the RCC continues:

> He will attack the mightiest fortresses with the help of a foreign god and will greatly honor those who acknowledge him. He will make them rulers over many people and will distribute the land at a price." (Daniel 11:39)

If you haven't read *The Early Church Father Catholic Fraud*, I suggest you read through the analysis that presents the RCC catechism—their operating manual—to help you understand a possible explanation for Daniel 11:39. Daniel has been focusing on the RCC and their spread in past visions, and there is no indication that the subject has changed. Therefore, as time winds down, it appears as though the RCC will join with a god considered by Christians to be a "foreign god." When we investigated the RCC catechism for *The Early Church Father Catholic Fraud*, we found interesting statements that stated their organization recognized the Muslim faith as having redeeming property that was equal to the saving grace of Jesus (Catechism #847 points to reference [337], LG16, that apparently makes this claim). Is this the foreign god that the RCC will use to expand their rule (He will attack the mightiest fortresses with the help of a foreign god and will greatly honor those who acknowledge him)? We can't be sure, but if the focus remains on the RCC which it seems to have been throughout these verses, then this is a real possibility for the future.

Next, we get to the time of the end that will have warring kingdoms from the South and North battling each other:

> "At the time of the end the king of the South will engage him in battle, and the king of the North will storm out against him with chariots and cavalry and a great fleet of ships. He will invade many countries and sweep through them like a flood. (Daniel 11:40)

As we found earlier, the North and the South are not with Jesus. The South is likely the consortium of the RCC and the governments of the world who have joined with the devil (king of the South will engage him in battle). The North will fight against them but, in the end, the devil will win (He will invade many countries and sweep through them like a flood).

We continue reading and we find more clues:

> He will also invade the Beautiful Land. Many countries will fall, but Edom, Moab, and the leaders of Ammon will be delivered from his hand. (Daniel 11:41)

The devil will smother the kingdom of God on earth (He will also invade the Beautiful Land). We need to understand the significance of Edom, Moab, and the leaders of Ammon to understand this passage, and we find that these are all countries opposed to God. Those who are spared are not with God—they are the opposition—and this indicates the angels of God are losing the spiritual battle on earth. We get more details:

> He will extend his power over many countries;
> Egypt will not escape. He will gain control of the
> treasures of gold and silver and all the riches of
> Egypt, with the Libyans and Cushites in submis-
> sion. But reports from the east and north will
> alarm him, and he will set out in a great rage to
> destroy and annihilate many. (Daniel 11:42–44)

The devil will spread his evil throughout the world and gain wealth and power. There will be one last stand for those who are aligned with the church of Jesus Christ (But reports from the east) and even some from those who were previously work-ing with the devil will join the side of Jesus (and north will alarm him). But this will enrage the devil (and he will set out in a great rage to destroy and annihilate many). As you can see, however, as we near the time of the end the ability to worship Jesus will continue to deteriorate as the forces of evil attempt to stomp out God from society.

This verse corresponds to the final remaining followers of Jesus:

> He will pitch his royal tents between the seas at
> the beautiful holy mountain. Yet he will come
> to his end, and no one will help. (Daniel 11:45)

The devil will spread throughout the world and the church, and it will appear as though God has left for good, and the devil has won (He will pitch his royal tents between the seas as the beautiful holy mountain). However, evil will not prevail, be-cause in the end, God will destroy evil (Yet he will come to his end). Nothing will change the time of the end when God takes back his creation, punishes evil (and no one will help), then establishes his eternal church. Daniel has just been presented an entire video of the future, but the video will not be complete unless we learn what happens to those who fought for evil and those who followed Jesus. Those details are presented next.

CHAPTER 20

Time of the End

*I*ATTENDED A SERMON RECENTLY with the pastor stating that many theologians and preachers believe that there will be a rapture in the time of the end for all followers of Jesus who are still alive at that time. He continued to clarify that it really doesn't matter whether a person believes in the one-time rapture or not because scripture tells us that we will all have a meeting with Jesus the moment we die. I bring this up because the last chapter in Daniel tells readers a bit about that last meeting with Jesus at the end of time and it emphasizes the importance of being right with Jesus in preparation for this impending meeting. Chapter twelve—the last chapter in Daniel—is all about the time of the end. We don't nearly have as many details of the time of the end in the book of Daniel as are presented in the book of Revelation, but what is presented is fascinating and warrants a close look.

Chapter twelve starts out by giving us more information about the angel that is with Daniel (Daniel 10:21) to guide people to follow the Lord:

> "At that time Michael, the great prince who protects your people, will arise. There will be a time of distress such as has not happened from the beginning of nations until then. But at that time your people—everyone whose name is found

written in the book—will be delivered. (Daniel
12:1)

If you are a Christian, you have heard of the book of life, and
your name is written in it. The opening verse in chapter twelve
informs us that the book of life is real, and we need to carefully
consider the contents of what's in it. First, the messenger tells
Daniel that there is an angel named Michael who protects the
people of God and, at the time of the time of the end, Michael
has a role to fill (Michael, the great prince who protects your
people, will arise). At the time of the end there will be pain
and agony at a severity never felt before (There will be a time
of distress such as not happened from the beginning of nations
until then). Think about that last statement and consider what
will be worse than wars, nuclear bombs, natural disasters, and
devastating illnesses we face on earth? Only one thing comes to
my mind and that is judgment and condemnation. Based on this
fact, Daniel 12:1 *must be* presenting what happens *after* that
final battle on earth—the spiritual battle on earth has ended.

Those who have followed the Lord are in for an eternity of
peace (But at that time your people —everyone whose name
is found written in the book—will be delivered). This is the
promise to Jeremiah that will be fulfilled. The path to redemption for God's people has just been revealed—the people of
the Lord will have their names written in the book of life and,
therefore, will live after their physical death on earth. Daniel is
in 535 BC, seventy years after God promised Jeremiah that the
people of God will be redeemed, and Daniel has just received
the answer to the promise. However, there is another aspect to
the time of the end—those who have been following evil will

face eternal punishment and this is the worst experience that anyone will ever have.

Daniel receives more details:

> Multitudes who sleep in the dust of the earth will awake: some to everlasting life, others to shame and everlasting contempt. Those who are wise will shine like the brightness of the heavens, and those who lead many to righteousness, like the stars for ever and ever. (Daniel 12:2–3)

Many who have died and will die (Multitudes who sleep in the dust of the earth) will rise (will awake) and be separated— some will be redeemed (some to everlasting life) and some to be condemned (others to shame and everlasting contempt). This does not claim that everyone who dies in the future will sleep in the dust. We learn from Revelation and other scripture that during the New Covenant those who follow Jesus will immediately hear the voice of Jesus when they die, and they will be called home to spend eternity in heaven with God. On the flip side, those who reject Jesus are immediately condemned by God. We will go into this concept in much greater detail when we review the book of Revelation, so with that as a teaser, we'll move on and continue with what's documented in Daniel. Those who live for God (Those who are wise) will radiate with life like how the angels have appeared to Daniel in his visions (will shine like the brightness of the heavens).

The messenger informs Daniel that his visions will not easily be understood:

But you, Daniel, roll up and seal the words of
the scroll until the time of the end. Many will go
here and there to increase knowledge." (Daniel
12:4)

The words of this scroll will be sealed up for most people
(roll up and seal the words of the scroll until the time of the
end) because they will be looking in the wrong places for answers (Many will go here and there to increase knowledge).
As we have already stated several times, people try to explain
prophecy through history rather than focusing on the spiritual
battle that is ongoing. When I started this review into prophecy over a year ago, the Holy Spirit unlocked the key for me
through the following simple vision:

- February 7, 2022—". . . the book of Revelation is not
  about the end of the world, it is only about the Church."
- February 9, 2022—". . . the book of Revelation is *all* about
  the church."

As I was starting my investigation into prophecy, I was told
twice that the book of Revelation is *all* about the church—not
partially about the church—it's *all about the church*. Of course,
this investigation was expanded into Daniel with the same basis for the understanding of both these prophetic books—it's
all about the church. How's that for some direction and help?
The Holy Spirit was telling me that if I focus on the relationship between God and people, the meaning of prophecy will be
provided to me.

Initially, I had no idea how valuable this one small bit of
direction obtained from these two visions was to help me

understand the message of prophecy. Daniel was told that the scroll would be sealed to "the time of the end" but it was also explained why—theologians and pastors will be looking outside of the church for answers. Jesus is the church of the New Testament and the entire Bible points to Jesus, therefore, how can the seventy sevens be interpreted to mean anything else other than Jesus? Every verse in Daniel applies to Jesus and the church, therefore, with that understanding the seal of Daniel is opened.

Daniel is near the end of the vision and there is only one question remaining:

> Then I, Daniel, looked, and there before me stood two others, one on this bank of the river and one on the opposite bank. One of them said to the man clothed in linen, who was above the waters of the river, "How long will it be before these astonishing things are fulfilled?" (Daniel 12:5–6)

The Word of God is like the water flowing in the river and there are people standing on both sides of this Word of God. I believe that both are representatives of people who have found and followed God because they are both next to the river and the representative of God is hovering over them both. I considered that this might indicate that even though there will be multiple interpretations of scripture (one on this bank of the river and one on the opposite bank), following the Word of God through scripture (the man clothed in linen, who is above the waters of the river) will redeem people.

One of the beings on one side of the river of life is asked about the timing of the time of the end (How long will it be before these astonishing things are fulfilled?):

> The man clothed in linen, who was above the waters of the river, lifted his right hand and his left hand toward heaven, and I heard him swear by him who livers forever, saying, "It will be for a time, times and half a time. When the power of the holy people has been finally broken, all these things will be completed." (Daniel 12:7)

The representative of Jesus (The man clothed in linen, who was above the waters of the river) looks up to the God of heaven for an answer to the question about how long will it be until the time of the end and judgment. At first, it appears as though Jesus provides a nonspecific answer (It will be for a time, times and half a time) but that is not the case because we know that the reference of *a time, times and half a time* means that there is a set time. The time of the end will be when the spirit of the church that Jesus and the disciples started has been broken (When the power of the holy people has been finally broken, all these things will be completed.). Earlier we stated that Daniel 11:45 indicates that at the time of the end there isn't much of the church left, and Revelation 20:8–9 verifies this by revealing that at the time of the end, the church will be in a "camp" and those attacking it will number like the "sand on the seashore." It certainly appears as though spiritual battle is overwhelming and "the power of the holy people has been finally broken" during this last battle between good and evil. Evil will win out over

the church on earth, but the good of God wins with the immediate arrival of the eternal church.

Daniel didn't understand this, so he tells the angel that he is
confused:

> I heard, but I did not understand. So I asked,
> "My lord, what will the outcome of all this be?"
> He replied, "Go your way, Daniel, because the
> words are rolled up and sealed until the time of
> the end. Many will be purified, made spotless,
> and refined, but the wicked will continue to be
> wicked. None of the wicked will understand,
> but those who are wise will understand. (Daniel
> 12:8–10)

I'm glad to hear that Daniel was confused because so was
I—then I prayed and focused on asking the Lord to provide
answers and the answers came. In response to Daniel's question, the Lord again tells Daniel that his understanding of the
meaning of this vision will be sealed up until the time of the
end. Daniel will not understand the meaning of this vision until the end of his life, but the message is not a difficult one to
understand. The messenger informs Daniel of the message of
the scroll—the connection to his last vision that he will receive
at the end of his life—the reference to the seventy sevens—the
Messiah—the one who will purify. The Lord has just told Daniel
that he will not understand this message until the end of his
life when the Lord provides Daniel with the rest of the details.
And what are these details? The Messiah will replace the daily
sacrifice with a one-time sacrifice that will save the multitudes

by purifying them of their sin (Many will be purified, made spotless, and refined). This part of Daniel 12:8–12 directly corresponds to the vision of 522 BC when the angel Gabriel will tell Daniel:

- "I have come to give you insight and understanding" (Daniel 9:22)
- "Seventy sevens are decreed for you people and your holy city to finish transgression, to put an end to sin to atone for wickedness, to bring in everlasting righteousness" (Daniel 9:24)
- "put an end to sacrifice and offering" (Daniel 9:27)

In 535 BC, the scroll was sealed up, but in 522 BC the seal is opened, and Daniel is provided the meaning of this vision.

But the sad part of this whole story is the devastation that Daniel was told about in the opening verse of chapter twelve—many people will not understand, and they are headed for the worst time ever experienced by anyone throughout all time—they will be condemned for not understanding and believing. The scroll has been unsealed and the message of Jesus is clear (Many will be purified, made spotless, and refined), but many will ignore it (but the wicked will continue to be wicked).

As this prophetic message is winding down, God's representative—the man in linen—provides the important message from Jesus; the keys to become purified, made spotless, and refined:

> From the time that the daily sacrifice is abolished and the abomination that causes desolation is set up, there will be 1,290 days. Blessed is

the one who waits for and reaches the end of the
1,335 days. (Daniel 12:11–12)

The connection to the seventy sevens couldn't be presented
any clearer. We have already analyzed these two passages and
provided their meaning, so there isn't any benefit in repeating the analysis. In summary, these two numbers provide the
founding of the church of Jesus Christ, therefore, God gave us
the church to help us learn about how Jesus purifies, makes
spotless, and refines all people. Jesus replaced the sin sacrifice
and started the church through the disciples who were blessed
for witnessing everything Jesus did. The visions of Daniel end
with this last message to ensure you know and understand the
most important message of prophecy—Jesus came for you and
all you need to do is believe this fact and you will receive your
reward in the end. God gave us the church as his kingdom on
earth to help us follow the path to heaven and the wise will
recognize this.

As an example of going here and there to increase knowledge rather than looking towards Jesus and his church for the
meaning of prophecy, I present the following explanation of
Daniel 12:11–12 from the NIV Study Bible:

> 12:11–12 Apparently representing either (1)
> further calculations relating to the persecutions
> by Antiochus Epiphanes (see 8:14; 11:28 and
> notes) or (2) further end-time calculations.

What?! Really?! The numbers that present the beautiful story of the start of the church of Jesus Christ —the most important
prophecy ever written—has been misconstrued because people

are looking here and there rather than looking at Jesus who is right in front of us all the whole time and present throughout our life and in the world. As I write this I am struggling with more rejection from the church because what I write is based on following Jesus and, in some cases, this contradicts years of teaching tradition in the church. I pray for it to end, but I'm feeling hopeless.

In closing, the message is simple—focus on Jesus and only Jesus and you will get answers. Look here and there and you miss the beautiful and obvious messages embedded in prophecy. The books of Daniel and Revelation are all about the church and the church is all about Jesus. If theological interpretations don't support the story of Jesus and the church, then they are in error and should be reevaluated—end of story. I can tell you in advance that our follow-up book that will interpret the book of Revelation will also be all about Jesus and his church.

The angel ends this vision by telling Daniel to rest because he will receive his reward:

> "As for you, go your way till the end. You will rest, and then at the end of the days you will rise to receive your allotted inheritance." (Daniel 12:13)

Daniel is told that he is to continue to do the king's work until he dies, then after he dies, he will rest for a while. After this rest he will rise to receive his reward—an inheritance. An inheritance is not something that is earned—it is a precious gift that someone passes on to you. With the sacrifice of Jesus, we have all received an unearned gift of salvation. However, this gift is only passed on to you if you become a member of the family of Jesus. Jesus gave us his church to learn how to become a family member. The wise will find Jesus and place him in their heart, but those who are wicked will remain wicked. The wise will be separated from the wicked for eternity.

The first time I wrote the draft of this last chapter I saved the file and the file saved was 333 kilobytes of data. I noted the 333 as the trinity of God three times and I thought, "Wow, God, you are so awesome!" I'm now at the end of the message the Holy Spirit has asked me to deliver; we have concluded our deep dive into Daniel and will close our message in the following chapter.

CHAPTER 21

It's All about Jesus

WHEN DIRECTORS OF MOVIES and TV productions are happy with a scene that they are filming, they shout out, "It's a wrap!" At the beginning of our review of Daniel we stated that our goal was to provide a thorough and accurate interpretation of this approximately 2,600-year-old prophetic book. Through the Holy Spirit's guidance and direction, we have now completed our review—it's a wrap! As we start this closing chapter it's appropriate to briefly summarize what we have found:

God—

- made permanent unbreakable promises, also called "decrees," with his creation of people,
- those who live according to God's commands will find eternal life and peace in his presence for eternity,
- those who reject God will, for eternity, experience pain and agony that is beyond anything ever felt on earth and this grief and will last eternity--it will never end (including separation from God),
- decreed specific periods of years for his kingdom on earth and each era or reign has a set start and ending (kingdom of gold, kingdom of silver, reign of the beast, and reign of Jesus),

- set the exact time for the arrival of the person he would bless the world through—his Son, Jesus the Messiah, and
- decreed seven years of protected time for the Messiah to complete his mission to replace the daily sacrifice requirements with his one-time sacrifice, then start his church—the bridge to help people find and follow Jesus,
- supports his angels to help the people of God navigate through the ongoing spiritual battle between good and evil, and,
- provides course corrections through his angels and other people to help steer people to find the grace of God.

The book of Daniel ended with a promise that the wise will understand the saving grace of Jesus promised to the world and communicated through the church of Jesus Christ (Daniel 12:11–12). Daniel was promised that he would live again because he lived his life in the family of God. How did Daniel join the family of God? Through daily contact with God—prayer together with a dedication to live according to the written word of God he learned about through the temple preachers. But what about the fulfillment of this promise? That brings us to the fulfillment of the last promise to Daniel (Daniel 12:13); did Daniel receive his inheritance or is he still resting while he waits for it?

If you've ever wondered about the details of the fulfillment of God's promise of eternal salvation for those in the Old Testament who followed the will of God, I am keeping company with you because I have also wondered. As I was getting ready to develop the first draft of the final chapter of this book, I prayed for guidance for that message of "It's a wrap." Can you guess how my prayer was answered? Of course, you can—the same way this book was started—with a vision. In response to my prayer, I received the following vision early in the morning of January 20, 2023:

> Karen and I entered a pub that was also a brewery of their own label of beer and we sat down to look at the menu. My eyes were immediately taken to a listing for their own brew of beer that I couldn't quite tell the name of, but was shocked to see the outrageous price of $27.53 for a glass. I'm not a connoisseur of beer but I couldn't help but wonder why this beer was priced so high. I ended up having two regular beers for $2.50 each; then Karen, like usual, because of my hearing problem, went up and paid the bill. I met her and, as we started walking out, she stated that she was shocked that the bill was $55.00 for two beers. She didn't want to argue with the bar patron and as I thought about it and was ready to go back to clear things up, I woke up.

This vision woke me up at 1:00 a.m. and I knew I had a lot of writing to do, but I tried to go back to sleep and laid in bed pondering that vision—What did it mean? I kept wondering. A while later, the vision was still on my mind; so, I knew it was time to get up to try to figure out what I had just been told.

I quickly realized that Karen and I rarely visit a pub because I'm really not a beer drinker. This is important, because it made no sense that I would be in a pub drinking beer and certainly wouldn't have been considering a $27.53 glass of beer. Then, I

started thinking about the numbers in the vision and they didn't make sense as two beers would not have been $55, or $27.50 each, it would have been $55.06 plus tax. With this in mind, I wondered if there was a scriptural connection to the numbers in the vision like I have experienced several times in the past. I typed 27:53 into an Internet search and up popped links to a verse of scripture that never sat right with me. Not surprisingly it was another one of those verses that had me questioning the truth and validity of scripture. I guess it was time to solve this mystery and even possibly have some direction for the book ending.

All the links that were on my search page pointed me to the following scripture:

> and coming out of the tombs after his resurrec-
> tion, they entered the holy city and appeared to
> many. (Matthew 27:53)

This passage of scripture always struck me as very weird because the author of the Gospel of Matthew was the only one of the four Gospel authors who wrote about this event. This event was so spectacular that I wondered in the past why the other authors hadn't captured such an important and mind-blowing major event. In fact, only having one author record this was just another reason to doubt the validity of the Gospels and the story of Jesus. Uh oh . . . here's that doubt again . . . and this doubt, like the others, was not seen as unfounded.

However, since my investigation results have eliminated all my doubts, I no longer looked at this passage as I would have in the past. Instead of wondering about whether it really happened, I thought it to be undoubtably true and, therefore, it was up to me to figure out why Nicodemus included this in his summary of Jesus. Did he witness this or was it included because the Holy Spirit had a message for him to record for future readers? I thought the answer to be yes!!! As I stated, I was not charged for *exactly* two house beers that were $27.53 each, I was charged $27.50, so I wondered if I was supposed to consider passages from Matthew 27:50–53 to put the message into context. This section of scripture did just that:

> Jesus cried again with a loud voice, and yielded up his spirit. Behold, the veil of the temple was torn in two from the top to the bottom. The earth quaked and the rocks were split. The tombs were opened, and many bodies of the saints who had fallen asleep were raised; and coming out of the tombs after his resurrection, they entered into the holy city and appeared to many. (Matthew 27:50–53)

The connection between the prices and the total scripture was now obvious. Hmm . . . I thought . . . I've just been through the book of Daniel that provided the prophecy of the coming of Jesus and how his mission was the bridge between the Old Covenant and the New Covenant—Jesus was the transition. Jesus as the transition between the Old and New Covenants was the focus of Daniel's book and now my vision has taken me directly to the moment of transition—the sacrifice. It couldn't be a coincidence, so I pondered what the Lord was trying to tell me while thinking to myself, "Isn't it amazing how God works?"

I needed both numbers to get the whole context of what the Lord wanted me to see, and the story helped me put the vision together. Had the Lord given me just numbers, I would have gone back to sleep. The Lord gave me a puzzle, and that got my attention!

Back to solving the puzzle— in the Matthew scripture, Nicodemus, a religious leader who wrote the Gospel of Matthew to prove Jesus was the Messiah, wrote that "many bodies of the saints" came out of the graves and "entered into the holy city" and "appeared to many." Nicodemus was a smart guy who focused on the theological aspects of the mission and sacrifice of Jesus. Did Nicodemus see these bodies or was he providing us an inspired message? The answer is "Yes." Nicodemus saw that through the sacrifice of Jesus, those people who lived according to the law of God through the Old Covenant—the saints—had just found their way home. They were being called home to the eternal kingdom of God. Nicodemus had written a message of hope in a world full of violence, turmoil, and death and it was likely based on a vision because it wasn't recorded by the other Gospel authors.

This book started with a vision that described my work as a soldier of the Lord to help bring people to faith. This book is now ending with a vision that provides the end results of this work—the promise of God for the redemption of Daniel who was one of God's people, was fulfilled. The message is that we can believe God's promise of eternal salvation and put our hope and faith in it. It was proven for Daniel and the rest of the Old Testament people of God who dedicated themselves to following the law and repenting of their sin. It was fitting that this book, which started with a vision, should end with a message derived from another vision. The promise God made to Daniel as he was making the ending statement in his book, was that "It's a wrap—it's a done deal—I *will* receive my inheritance," and this was proven in Nicodemus' vision of the transition between the Old and New Covenants as Jesus made his one-time sacrifice.

Christians sing songs and continuously praise God for being faithful and keeping his promises. Theologians have for years claimed that many of the promises God provided to Daniel have been fulfilled, however, the full story is that *all the promises* made to Daniel have been fulfilled—including his rest and resurrection—except for one—the promise of the eternal church. We have been through every verse of Daniel and every promise that God made in this book has been fulfilled except for the coming of the eternal kingdom of Jesus. This is a strong foundation to look forward to and if you have been following Jesus, take comfort in knowing you have made the right choice. If you haven't been following Jesus, I hope this book has helped take you one step closer to doing so.

The bus was called for you to get on it and see the truth in scripture that points to Jesus. Don't worry about all the confusion and the corruption in the church because you can't do anything about it. As Daniel was told, the wicked will continue to be wicked and that is not our concern. What is our responsibility is to expose the corruption and evil presence in the church that points them to the wrong bus and/or helps them get on the wrong bus. As stated at the beginning of this book, my job is to address this confusion and deception and help others get on the right bus.

Just when I thought I had enough to end this book, I had another vision to close out this book with:

> February 5, 2023—I was removing a door from our white Toyota Sienna van, but it was too heavy and got a bit out of my control. As I tried to control the door, it slid across a three-to-four-feet section of the van and made a deep scratch in it. The scratch was only visible to me if I took a very close look at it; otherwise, it was hidden from view.

Not everyone will see the damage to the church that I see and have reported on. We addressed this early on in our introduction to my visions that needed prayer and time to understand. If the Lord is talking to you and showing you the damage in the church and that's all you see—don't sit on your hands staring at it—dig into scripture and find an answer. If you don't see the damage in the church, then God has blessed you with a sealed vision and there is nothing wrong with that—except I ask one thing of you—try to understand us who see the deep scratch—the effects of false teachers. Those of us who think differently and only see the corruption of the church need to be understood and welcomed into the church. My job is to help these people find Jesus through the imperfections in the church and your job is to support this process. Do not look at someone who sees the scratch as working for the devil—approach them with kindness and have an intelligent facts-based discussion.

Although you don't see the damage to the white van—it is there—Jesus warned you about it and the apostles extensively addressed it. God provided us the scripture and course corrections that are like magic in our lives to seek and find Jesus, but we are all human. The disciples were human, Daniel was human, the theologians are human, and those who corrupted the Gospel and continue to corrupt the church are human. The Holy Spirit has been talking to every human, but the Holy Spirit doesn't always get through. That great ongoing spiritual battle that Daniel addressed in his closing vision is the one that we are all in and fighting—whether you want to participate or not—if you are a Christian, you are in the battle—like it or not.

If you have not asked God for forgiveness for your sins yet, you are living on borrowed time because your life will, one day, permanently end; and, you will know the truth. The choice for eternal peace or an eternity of pain so great and dreadful that it exceeds anything ever witnessed on earth should be a strong incentive to change your ways and embrace the truth. With the details of Daniel completely laid out, there is no doubt that the promise of eternity will be kept. Consider your life and the course corrections God has already provided you to seek him out. Compare your life to the life you are expected to live as a God-created human and, if you are not following the Word of God through Jesus, use prayer and determination to change your course before it is too late. Don't be a gambler and bet on this life being the end of it all—because you will lose that bet.

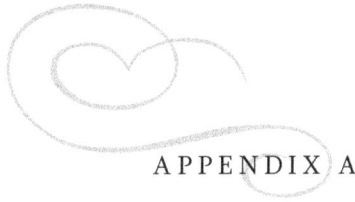

Time Line of Daniel's Life

Estimate year of Daniel's birth	c.615 BC
Nebuchadnezzar invades Judah and takes Daniel hostage	605 BC
Nebuchadnezzar's reign	605–561 BC
Daniel enters training for three years	604–601 BC
Daniel enters as a wise man into Nebuchadnezzar's service	601 BC
Daniel remains in the service of the kings as a wise man	601–539 BC
Daniel's second year of service, Nebuchadnezzar has a statue dream	600 BC
Daniel is promoted to manager of the wise men	600 BC
Nebuchadnezzar builds an enormous pagan gold statue	600–598 BC
Daniel's friends are thrown into a hot furnace and survive	597 BC
Nebuchadnezzar's dream of the tree of life	595 BC
Nebuchadnezzar dream is fulfilled as he is punished	594 BC
Nebuchadnezzar is restored to his kingdom and turns to God	592 BC
Nebuchadnezzar dies	561 BC
Babylonian King Merodach	561–560 BC
Babylonian King Neriglissar	559–556 BC
Babylonian King Marduk	556 BC
Babylonian King Nabonidus	555–542 BC
Babylonian King Belshazzar	542–539 BC
Daniel's vision of the New Covenant with a focus on the beast	541 BC

Daniel interprets the writing on the wall for Belshazzar	539 BC
Daniel is promoted to the third-highest ruler in the kingdom	539 BC
Belshazzar is executed and replaced by the Persian King Cyrus	539–530 BC
Daniel's vision of the New Covenant with focus on the ram and goat	539 BC
Daniel's vision of the future—fulfills Jeremiah's seventy-year promise	535 BC
Persian King Cambyses II	530–522 BC
Persian King Bardiya	522 BC
Persian King Darius	522–486 BC
Daniel survives the lion's den	522 BC
Daniel's vision of the coming Messiah	522 BC
Daniel writes his story, the book of Daniel	522 BC

Time Line of the Covenant and Kingdom

1	Eternity	Jesus Exists	Jesus is, was, and always will be (Daniel 9:25).
2	c. 2000–2330	God's kingdom on earth	Creation and the people of God: Began with the covenant between God and Abraham and continues through to the time of the end.
3	c.2000 BC–AD 30	The Old Covenant of the Law	God's decree for salvation through animal sacrifices; starts with Abraham, through Moses, then ends with the sacrifice of Jesus.
	592–561 BC	Kingdom of gold	Nebuchadnezzar is the kingdom of gold (Daniel 2:38).
	561 BC–AD 30	Kingdom of silver	The "kingdom of silver" consisting mostly of pagan kingdoms who do not worship the one true God (Daniel 2:39, 7:2, 10:20–11:30). This is an "inferior" kingdom.
	439/440 BC	Malachi's prediction of the coming of the Messiah	The last prophecy of the Old Testament (Malachi 3:1). After Malachi, prophecy goes silent (Daniel 9:24).
	5/6 BC	The arrival of the Messiah as predicted by Malachi	Jesus (the seven sevens) is born 434 years (sixty-two sevens) after Malachi documented the prophecy of the coming of Jesus (Daniel 9:25).

4	26–33 BC	Transition	The seven of Jesus (see Appendix C). This is the kingdom that will never be destroyed set up during the kingdoms of silver and bronze (Daniel 2:44, 4:10–12).
5	AD 30–2330	The New Covenant of Jesus	The "end times" or "hour" of the New Covenant of Jesus, and the kingdom of iron that will never be destroyed (Daniel 2:44–45, 4:40–43, 9:27, Romans 10:12). It will be a mixed kingdom that is split between the beast and the reign of Jesus (Daniel 8:2–14; 11:31–39; 1 John 2:18–19; Luke 21:24).
	AD 30–1330*	The first part of the split covenant called the reign of the beast and the kingdom of bronze	The reign of the beast—the RCC (Daniel 2:39, 7:3-8, Revelation 12:7-13:18). The RCC controls the words of Jesus and the church for 1,300 years.
	AD 1330–2330	Jesus returns to earth	The reign of Jesus over his church (Daniel 3:9–11). Jesus returns to earth to free his words from the control of false teachers and reign over his church. (Daniel 7:9–12; Revelation 8:1, 20:4).
6	2330–eternity	The eternal kingdom —the rock that smashes	The rock that smashes all the other kingdoms on earth (Daniel 2:45)—the eternal kingdom of Jesus with his eternal church arrives for God to always be with his people (Daniel 7:13–14, 7:27, 8:13–14; Revelation 21:1–3).

The "Seven" of Jesus

1.	AD 26–30	The first half of the "seven" of Jesus—preaching, teaching, and healing for 1,260 days while being protected by God (Daniel 9:24–27, Revelation 12:1–6). Jesus and the disciples are protected from harm during this period (Daniel 9:26–27; Mark 14:41; John 2:4, 7:6, 12:23, 17:12; Revelation 12:1–6).
2.	AD 30	In the middle of the "seven" the Anointed One will be put to death (Daniel 9:27). The forty-five-days (1335–1290) of those who will be blessed (Daniel 12:11–12) to see the transition from the Old Covenant to the New Covenant, also called *the start of the "end times"*—the time of Jesus (1 John 2:18–19) and the commissioning of the start of the church (Matthew 28:18–20). This time will last for 2,300 years (Daniel 8:14).
3.	Five days	There were five days set aside for the replacement of the sacrifice that consisted of Jesus' execution, three days in the grave, rising from the dead to appear to the disciples, and the ascension back to heaven (from all four Gospels and calculated from Daniel 9:24–27, 12:11–12 and Revelation 12:6).

4.	Forty days	Forty days of appearances of Jesus together with the disciples receiving the Holy Spirit (Acts 1:3–7, Daniel 12:11–12) and the commissioning from Jesus for the disciples to start the church (Matthew 28:16–20). We know that at that time, even though Jesus appeared for forty days, some disciples still doubted (Matthew 28:16–17). The disciples are welcomed into the New Covenant by Jesus when the Holy Spirit is breathed into them during an appearance by Jesus after his resurrection (John 20:22).
5.	AD 30	The abomination of desolation—the church is evacuated by the religious leaders who refused to accept Jesus as the sacrifice. They vacated the temple then persecuted and even executed the followers of Jesus and the leaders of the church (Revelation 17:12, 17–18; Daniel 9:27, 11:31, 12:11).
6.	AD 30–33	The Holy Spirit is breathed into the Jews to usher in the New Covenant of Jesus promised by Joel (Acts 2:1–21). The last half of the "seven" of Jesus fulfills Daniels prophecy of the "seven sevens" (Daniel 9:27). The last half of the "seven" of Jesus lasted for 1,290 days (Daniel 9:26–27, 12:11–12). The disciples were protected from harm during this time (Revelation 12:9), but the church was immediately infiltrated and attacked by false teachers (Acts 1:1–6:7). The sacrifice of Jesus in AD 30 ushered in the "abomination that causes desolation" (Daniel 9:26–27, 11:31) but it wasn't completely "set up" until 1,290 days after the sacrifice was abolished (Daniel 12:11).
7.	AD 33	The disciples who witnessed the 1,335 days of Jesus are blessed (Daniel 12:12) because they were the only people who ever lived that participated in the five days of the sacrifice (five days), witnessed the appearances of Jesus after he rose from the dead (forty days), and then performed their assigned job to start the church (1,290 days).

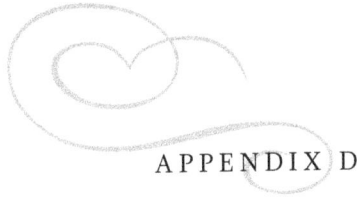

Time Line of Scripture References in Daniel

Citation	Year (BC)	Ruler	Description
Chapter 1	615		Estimated year of Daniel's birth
Chapter 1	605	Nebuchadnezzar	Daniel is abducted and taken captive by the Babylonian king during the Babylonian siege of Judah.
1:5, 1:13	604–601	Nebuchadnezzar	Daniel starts training for three years to enter King Nebuchadnezzar's service. We have assumed that Daniel immediately started training.
1:18–19, 2:18	601	Nebuchadnezzar	Daniel is released into the service of King Nebuchadnezzar as a wise man.
1:21	601–539	Various Babylonian Kings from history	Daniel remains as a wise man in the king's service for a few years. Then, he is promoted to manager of the wise men until the first year of the Persian King Cyrus.
2:1	600	Nebuchadnezzar	In Daniel's second year as a subject under King Nebuchadnezzar, this king has a vision of a statue.

2:29–45	600	Nebuchadnezzar	Daniel interprets Nebuchadnezzar's dream of a statue and demands the whole kingdom worship it. Nebuchadnezzar is named as the head of gold in the kingdom of gold—the kingdom of gold begins. • Four or five kingdoms and two transitions can be considered during the covenant with God. • Nebuchadnezzar is the first kingdom—the gold.
2:48	600	Nebuchadnezzar	Nebuchadnezzar rewards Daniel for revealing and interpreting his dream by promoting him to manager of all the wise men of the kingdom.
3:1	600–598	Nebuchadnezzar	The course correction dream of Nebuchadnezzar did not convert him to follow God—he builds a very large pagan statue of gold for his whole kingdom to worship.
3:19–22	597	Nebuchadnezzar	Daniel's Jewish friends refuse to worship the pagan statue and are thrown into the very hot furnace. They survive, thereby providing another course correction to Nebuchadnezzar, but this also fails to convert the king.

4:1–18	595	Nebuchadnezzar	Then, Nebuchadnezzar has a vision of a tree. It is estimated to have occurred a few years after the furnace fire because the effects of that course correction have worn off and this king has returned to his pagan ways. • It is a vision of the saving grace of the Messiah, but Daniel doesn't pick up on that. • Unless Nebuchadnezzar converts, he will get a devastating course correction that will temporarily remove his reign over the kingdom.
4:28	594	Nebuchadnezzar	Twelve months after the vision is interpreted, this king has not changed his ways; so, God fulfills the vision and Nebuchadnezzar goes into the wild and loses his mind.
4:33–37	592	Nebuchadnezzar	Nebuchadnezzar repents after God gives him this course correction and he fully turns to God to become the leader God wanted him to be—the "seven" years of this tree vision were not intended to refer to calendar years—in preparation for a vision he would receive later. God wanted Daniel to recognize that *seven* means complete and thorough.

History	561	Merodach	Nebuchadnezzar dies and the inferior kingdom of gold ends and the kingdom of silver begins.
2:39	561–542	Merodach, Neriglissar, Labasi, and Marduk	The rulers of the kingdom of silver are interior. From history we know there were four kings of Babylon during this time and Daniel does not mention any of them as following the Lord.
5:2	542	Belshazzar	A pagan descendent of Nebuchadnezzar eventually takes over the reign of the Babylonian kingdom, mocks God, then is later punished for it.
7:1	541	Belshazzar	In the "first year of Belshazzar," Daniel has a vision that captures all five kingdoms and the two transitions specified in the vision of the statue— • Jesus (the iron) will come to transition the kingdom of silver to the kingdom of bronze—the beasts, • that will be replaced by the reign of Jesus (iron/clay), • then the rock of Jesus will smash and transition the kingdom to the eternal church of Jesus.

8:1	539	Belshazzar	In the "third year of King Belshazzar's reign," Daniel has a vision about a ram and a goat—the complete picture of the two covenants and the transition between them. There will be a corrupted church, but the saving grace of Jesus will ultimately win for eternity.
5:1–5, 5:26–28	539	Belshazzar	Daniel interprets the writing on the wall for Belshazzar. According to the writing, Belshazzar will be executed and the kingdom of Babylon given to the Medes and Persians.
5:29	539	Belshazzar	Belshazzar rewards Daniel for his prediction of doom by making him the third-highest ruler in the kingdom.

5:30	539	Belshazzar	Persians invade the Babylonian kingdom, Belshazzar is killed, and King Cyrus takes over the kingdom.
1:21	539	Belshazzar/ Cyrus	Daniel is no longer with the wise men. He went to the wise men with Nebuchadnezzar, was promoted to manager, then remained with the wise men until the last day of the reign of Belshazzar when he was promoted to the third-highest ruler in the kingdom. This also happened to be the first year of the reign of Cyrus.
5:31	539	Cyrus	Daniel says that Darius takes over the kingdom, but this is in error. He meant Cyrus, who history can verify as sixty-two years old. The mistake was likely made because the next story Daniel provides has Daniel in the kingdom of Darius.

6:28	539–530	Cyrus	Daniel prospers—this king follows the God of heaven.
10:1	535	Cyrus	In the third year of Cyrus, king of Persia, seventy years after Jeremiah's prophecy, Daniel receives the answer to Jeremiah's promise—a vision of the complete future of the covenants of God. This is the third time that God has provided Daniel visions of the future of the covenants—but he still doesn't understand his visions.
History	530–522	Persian rulers	Historical Persian rulers between Cyrus and Danius
5:31	522–486	Darius and History	Darius the Mede takes over as ruler. Darius was born in 550 BC.
6:1	522	Darius	Darius is planning to set Daniel "over the whole kingdom."
6:2–27	522	Darius	Daniel is not harmed in the lion's den and Daniel is informed about the decree of the Medes and Persians that applies to God who has decreed eternal life for those who follow God.
6:28	522–486	Darius	Daniel prospers—King Darius follows the God of heaven at least while Daniel is still alive in 522 BC

9:1	522	Darius	"In the first year of Darius" Daniel is mourning near the end of his life because he has not yet seen the answer to Jeremiah's promise. He prays and pleads and in response an angel provides Daniel the "seventy sevens" vision predicting the coming of the Messiah and how the Messiah will fulfill Jeremiah. • The vision is all about Jesus. • With this vision near the end of Daniel's life, he now understands the meaning of the "seven" from the vision of the tree and can assemble his visions into a book

The "New Covenant"

HE "END TIMES" OR "hour of the New Covenant" of Jesus started in AD 30 with the replacement of animal sacrifice with the sacrifice of Jesus. This hour of heaven is set to expire 2,300 years later in the year AD 2330. The "New Covenant" will be a split kingdom consisting of the reign of the beast from AD 30–1330, then the return of Jesus to reign over the church from AD 1330–2330. This entire period will consist of a corrupted church that people will have to maneuver through to find Jesus (Daniel 6:8, 6:12, 6:15, 8:2–12; 11:31–39; 1 John 2:18–19; Revelation 21:1–3; Romans 10:12; Luke 21:24). Because of the corruption of the church, the New Covenant will not be a time of peace (Daniel 9:24–27). The church is corrupted from start to finish, therefore, this period of time is time of strife for those seeking Jesus.

1.	AD 30	The transition from the Old Covenant to the New Covenant with the coming of Jesus who will bring the kingdom that will never end (Daniel 2:44, 4:10–12, 8:2–4, 10:2–6, 11:31)
2.	AD 30	The false teachers and those who do not want Jesus to replace the temple sacrifice infiltrate the starting church (Acts 1:1–6:7).
3.	AD 30–1330	The "kingdom of bronze" (Daniel 2:39, 7:3–7, 7:23, 7:25, 10:1, 10:7–8)—the pretend kingdom also called "the reign of the beast" and "the RCC." The RCC controls the words of Jesus and the church for 1,300 years.

4.	AD 1330	A man named John Wycliffe is born. Wycliffe will be the first to translate the Bible into the language of the people to give all people the ability to find the true words of Jesus!
5.	AD 1330	The transition between the reign of the RCC and the reign of Jesus—the beast was removed from power but was not destroyed. It was allowed to continue to exist with other false churches (Daniel 7:12, 7:24) until the time of the end.
6.	AD 1330– 2330	The "kingdom of part iron and part clay" (Daniel 2:40–43)—also known as "the reign of Jesus over his church." The RCC will control the Word of God until Jesus returns to take over the church (Daniel 7:21–22, 7:26). During this period the church will be on fire for Jesus (Daniel 7:7–10; Revelation 8:1, 20:4).
7.	AD 2330	There will be a final battle with the many who are evil against the few remaining who follow good (Daniel 11:40–45).
8.	AD 2330	The books are opened and those who were prevented from hearing the words of Jesus during the reign of the RCC are judged for their actions and their words (Daniel 7:9–10, 12:1–3; Revelation 20:12–15).
9.	AD 2330– eternity	At the time of the end, the eternal church of Jesus Christ will start and it will never end (Daniel 2:44–45). The rock that smashes all the other kingdoms on earth (Daniel 2:45)—the eternal kingdom of Jesus with his eternal church—arrives for God to always be with his people (Daniel 7:13–14, 7:27, 8:13–14) and Revelation 21:1–2).